COLLECTOR'S EDITION

QUEEN ELIZABETH II

Diamond Jubilee

60 GLORIOUS YEARS

For Joe Little
Friend and Royal expert

Pedigree

Published 2012. Pedigree Books Ltd,
Beech Hill House, Walnut Gardens, Exeter, Devon EX4 4DH
books@pedigreegroup.co.uk I www.pedigreebooks.com
© Press Association Images

About the Author

Ian Lloyd has a degree in Medieval and Modern History from the University of Nottingham, as well as diplomas in photography, management and bookselling. He has been a professional writer and photographer for over twenty years and had produced articles for many UK magazines and newspapers including *Hello, Saga, Majesty, Radio Times, Classic FM Magazine*, the *Daily Mail*, the *Daily Express*, the *Daily Telegraph* and *The Sunday Times.* He is the Royal Correspondent for The Sunday Post and The People's Friend Magazine.

His books include *Crown Jewel: A Year in the Life of the Queen Mother* in 1989 and *William: The People's Prince in 2003.* In 2011 his book *William and Catherine: A Royal Wedding Album* reached number three in *The Sunday Times.* Bestseller List and *Invitation To The Royal Wedding* reached number ten. He also produced *Elizabeth Taylor: Queen of the Silver Screen.*

As a royal commentator he appears frequently on *Sky News, BBC News 24, BBC Breakfast, NBC, Fox News, Radio 5 Live, Radio Ulster* and *Radio Wales.* He has lectured on the Royal Family for Cunard, and is also an after dinner speaker.

He lives in Oxford. www.ianlloyd.co.uk

Contents

Princess Elizabeth wears a silver gown
with a diamond tiara and pearl necklace.
August 30, 1949.

INTRODUCTION

*When the future Elizabeth II was born
in April 1926 there was no expectation
she would be Queen.*

Her father, the Duke of York, was the second son of the King-Emperor George V and her mother was the popular 'smiling Duchess.' Her Uncle David was heir to the throne and would one day succeed Edward VIII. If, as was expected, he married and produced children, his own heirs would continue the dynasty. Elizabeth would be their cousin; a distant relative, carrying out royal engagements, the way the Duke of Kent and Princess Alexandra do today.

And then of course her mother, not yet aged 25 when the princess was born, could produce a succession of sons who would displace the young Elizabeth in the line of succession.

None of this was to be. The Duchess of York gave birth to only one other child, a daughter, Princess Margaret.

Then in 1936 Elizabeth's world was changed forever. She was just ten years old when her uncle, Edward VIII, abdicated after less than a year on the throne. Her father became King George VI and she herself became Heiress Presumptive.

The Second World War was declared in 1939 when she was thirteen and she and Margaret spent the next five years at Windsor Castle. When peace was declared their father King George wrote: "Poor darlings, they have never had any fun yet."

Among the occasional visitors was Elizabeth's distant cousin, Prince Philip of Greece. With his dazzling Viking good looks and charm he caught Elizabeth's eye and she fell in love with him and, according to all accounts, has remained in love with him ever since.

They were engaged in the summer of 1947 and married the following November. It was the first great royal ceremony since the war. It came at a time of rationing and austerity and Winston Churchill famously called it a "flash of colour on the hard road we have to travel."

Elizabeth became a mother at the age of 22 when she gave birth to Prince Charles, followed two years later by Princess Anne. These were happy, carefree years and Elizabeth was able to fly out to Malta for lengthy stays with Philip, who was based there with the Royal Navy.

Their idyllic way of life was tragically cut short. George VI was suffering from cancer and died aged just 56. Elizabeth succeeded to the throne aged 25 – the same age Elizabeth I was when she became Queen – and Philip, aged 30, was forced to abandon his promising naval career.

It is impossible for a younger generation to have any idea of the impact these two glamorous people had on the world stage. With her slim physique, blue eyes, peaches and cream complexion, and impeccable style, Elizabeth was the fairy tale princess and queen. Their early tours made an incredible impact on people. In Australia alone it was estimated that three-quarters of the country's population glimpsed her in the flesh on her first tour in 1953.

With her slim physique, blue eyes, peaches and cream complexion, and impeccable style, Elizabeth was the fairy tale princess and queen.

Elizabeth has become the most travelled monarch in British history and Philip has been beside her on every overseas tour.

In sixty years as monarch, Elizabeth II has never put a foot wrong. She was influenced by her parents and grandparents and has developed a style of monarchy that they would have understood and approved of. More importantly she has stayed true to the lessons and beliefs that were instilled in her at an early age. She has remained a reassuring constant in a world of change.

We see her image every day on coins and stamps as well as in the media and yet she still remains elusive. She is the most famous woman in the world and yet one of the most private. She has never given an interview and though she keeps a diary it will be decades hence before official biographers will be able to divulge some of its tantalising contents.

When she was a child she said she would like to grow up to be a lady living in the country with lots of horses and dogs. Instead her fate was to live a life on the public stage, where, for the past six decades, she has represented her country and the Commonwealth with dignity and regality, and will continue to do so for as long as she can.

A smiling Queen Elizabeth II waves from the Irish State coach as she drives to the House of Lords to open Parliament in London. This was the first time since 1886 that a Queen opened Parliament. November 4, 1951.

The Duchess of York (later the Queen Mother) with her husband the Duke of York (later George VI), and their daughter Princess Elizabeth at her christening. May 1926.

From Princess to Queen

1926 – 1952

*"Her Royal Highness the Duchess of York was safely
delivered of a Princess at 2:40am this morning,
Wednesday April 21" (1926).*

From Princess to Queen

The formal announcement was immediately telegraphed to all parts of the Empire ruled by the baby's grandfather, King George V. The king himself was in residence at Windsor Castle and had left instructions that he should be roused at any hour of the night as soon as the news came through. He was awoken at 4am with the glad tidings and later the same morning his consort, Queen Mary, wrote in her journal, "Such a relief and joy."

It was "a relief" since the birth hadn't been straightforward. A medical bulletin stated, "a certain line of treatment was successfully adopted," which was 1920s speak for a Caesarean section.

The future Elizabeth II was born at 17 Bruton Street, the Mayfair home of her maternal grandparents, the Earl and Countess of Strathmore. The end of Bruton Street was bombed during the Second World War completely destroying number 17. By coincidence the royal couturier, Norman Hartnell, who would design both Elizabeth's wedding dress and Coronation gown, would establish his studio across the road at number 26.

Although the baby was third in line to the throne, there was little likelihood that she would one day become Queen. The heir to the throne was her Uncle David, the hugely popular 31-year-old Prince of Wales, who was of course expected to marry in due course and, even more importantly, to raise a family.

The princess was the daughter of the prince's younger brother Prince Albert, Duke of York, known to his friends and family as 'Bertie' and his charismatic wife Elizabeth. The Yorks were married in April 1923 and Elizabeth proved the ideal soulmate for the shy and retiring prince who was also afflicted with a stammer, the outcome of childhood attempts to 'cure' his lefthandedness by forcing him to write with his other hand.

Elizabeth's natural charm and relaxed style endeared her to the press and public alike. She was dubbed 'the Smiling Duchess' and was a complete contrast to the shy and slightly formidable Queen Mary.

George and Mary were cold and authoritarian figures to their six children. The King's attitude to parenthood is best summed up by his oft-quoted remark to his friend Lord Derby, "My father was frightened of his mother. I was frightened of my father, and I'm damned well going to make sure that my children are frightened of me."

In contrast to Bertie, Elizabeth had an idyllic Edwardian childhood. She was the ninth of ten children and her parents, who became the 14th Earl and Countess of Strathmore in 1904, were warm and affectionate figures. The countess was known to bowl oranges and apples the length of the dining table to her cricket mad husband – something hard to imagine the occupants of Buckingham Palace indulging in.

Elizabeth was a natural homemaker and determined that Bertie and their children should enjoy the same happiness and security that had characterised her early life. The Duke was enchanted with his new daughter and wrote to his mother: "You don't know what a tremendous joy it is to Elizabeth and me to have our little girl. We always wanted a child to make our happiness complete, and now that it has happened, it seems so wonderful and strange."

The princess was christened 'Elizabeth Alexandra Mary' in the private chapel at Buckingham Palace on 29 May 1926. The choice of names had to be approved by the King. Elizabeth was of course her mother's name and, as Bertie pointed out, the name hadn't been used by the royal family "for such a long time." Alexandra was in memory of the King's mother, Alexandra of Denmark, the widow of King Edward VII, who had died at her beloved Sandringham House the previous November at the age of 81. Mary was the name of the Queen and also of Bertie's only sister who had married the future Earl of Harewood in 1922 and who had already provided the King with two grandsons.

Mary was one of the baby's godparents, along with the King and Queen, the Earl of Strathmore, Lady Elphinstone

Princess Elizabeth was christened in the Private Chapel of Buckingham Palace on 29 May 1926 by Cosmo Lang, Archbishop of York. Afterwards the baby's parents and godparents posed for this historic photo.

(L-R, back row) The Duke of Connaught, King George V, The Duke of York (later George VI) and The Earl Strathmore. (L-R, front row) Lady Elphinstone, Queen Mary, The Duchess of York (later the Queen Mother) with Princess Elizabeth, The Countess of Strathmore and Princess Mary.

The baby princess being pushed in the park by her nanny.
As she smiles at the camera she can have had little idea that
the rest of her life would be spent under its constant gaze.

– the Duchess's sister, and the Duke of Connaught. The latter was very much a link with the past. Born in 1850 he was Queen Victoria's favourite son and his own godfather had been the Duke of Wellington, the victor of the 1815 Battle of Waterloo. As a child the future Elizabeth II grew up knowing three of Victoria's children and, aged 18, attended the funeral of Princess Beatrice, the youngest (and last to die) of the Queen Empress's nine children.

The baby princess was put under the care of nanny Clara Knight, whose father was a tenant farmer on the Strathmore's estate at St Paul's Walden in Hertfordshire. Clara was originally the Duchess of York's nanny and was looking after the children of the Duchess's sister, Lady Elphinstone, before being head hunted to look after the new baby.

She soon became known to the Yorks as 'Alah' after the baby Elizabeth's early attempts at saying Clara. Another sobriquet based on the princess's mispronunciation is still in use today - the Queen is known to her closest family and friends as 'Lilibet' – her version of the name Elizabeth.

According to royal biographer, Robert Lacey, Alah was "an old-fashioned nanny, a family retainer in the traditional style, whose whole life was her work, welcoming the role of surrogate mother put on her by her employers, delighting in the challenge of coping with everything, and scarcely ever taking a holiday or even a day off."

With the help of a nursery maid she would feed and dress her little charge; making sure she looked her best for her twice daily meetings with her parents and cuddling her if she woke up during the night.

The nursery maid was Margaret MacDonald, who was soon rechristened 'Bobo' by the infant princess and would eventually become Elizabeth's dresser and closest confidante.

She would share a room with the princess until Elizabeth was eleven and she was the only below-stairs member of staff to ever call her 'Lilibet.' She looked after her charge for 67 years until her death in her rooms at Buckingham Palace in September 1993. Every year on Bobo's birthday the Queen would enjoy a rare role reversal and serve her loyal assistant breakfast in bed.

"In her later years, Bobo held a unique position in Buckingham Palace, having her own suite, no duties and enjoying a closer personal friendship with the queen than practically anyone else, including some of the queen's closest relatives," Douglas Keay wrote in his biography of the queen.

In the autumn of 1926 it was announced that the Yorks would undertake a six-month tour of Australia and New Zealand, during which the Duke would open the new Parliament building in Canberra. Today it seems an unnecessarily harsh decision of King George's to send the new parents to the other side of the world, especially as they would miss Elizabeth's first birthday.

The royal couple said goodbye to their daughter at London's Victoria Station on 6 January 1927. A few days later the Duchess of York wrote to her mother-in-law, Queen Mary: "I felt very much leaving... and the baby was so sweet playing with the buttons on Bertie's uniform that it quite broke me up."

The tour was a triumph and on their return on 27 June they appeared to the thousands of cheering people gathered outside Buckingham Palace, bringing Elizabeth out for her first appearance on the balcony overlooking the Mall.

Later in the day there would be another balcony appearance as the Yorks waved to the crowd from their new home 145 Piccadilly which they would lease as

Every year on Bobo's birthday the Queen would enjoy a rare role reversal and serve her loyal assistant breakfast in bed.

their London residence for almost ten years until their unexpected move to Buckingham Palace. Like 17 Bruton Street it too was destroyed by enemy fire during the War.

The royal nursery was on the top floor of the building. It was just visible from Buckingham Palace and at a prearranged time the princess would wave her handkerchief across to the palace and the King, dubbed 'Grandpapa England' by Lilibet, would wave his in reply.

The King fell seriously ill with bronchial pneumonia in 1928 and very nearly died. He was sent to recuperate in Bognor, West Sussex and in March he was greatly cheered by the arrival of Elizabeth who sat on his knee and joined him for walks on the seafront. At one point the Archbishop of Canterbury arrived to discover the king on all fours, playing horses with Lilibet who was patiently tugging him along by his beard.

Winston Churchill, who met the baby princess at this time, wrote to his wife "she is a character. She has an air of authority and reflectiveness astonishing in an infant."

In August 1930 the princess was joined in the nursery of 145 Piccadilly by a new sister. Upon hearing that the baby was to be called Margaret Rose, four year old Elizabeth announced, "I'm going to call her Bud," explaining to Lady Cynthia Asquith, "well she's not a real rose yet, is she?"

By this time the older princess was the world's darling. Her effigy appeared in Madame Tussauds on horseback and her face appeared on a five-cent stamp in Newfoundland. Hospital wards were named after her and part of Antarctica became known as Princess Elizabeth Land. A popular song was composed as a tribute and, aged only three, she made her first appearance on the cover of *Time* magazine.

In 1931 the King granted the Yorks the use of Royal Lodge in Windsor Great Park. The Queen Mother would continue to use it after the death of the King in 1952 and it was here that she died in 2002. Today it is the home of another Duke of York, Prince Andrew, the Queen's second son and two latter-day princesses of York: Beatrice and Eugenie.

In the grounds of Royal Lodge there still exists a tiny thatched cottage, *Y Bwthyn Bach*, a present from the

people of Wales given to Elizabeth on her sixth birthday. It featured all the mod cons of a 1930s middle class cottage all built at a specially reduced size. It is too small for an adult to stand upright in but it was the perfect play home for the two princesses.

That same spring, the nursery staff was joined by Scots born Marion Crawford, who was engaged as the royal governess despite being only 22.

With a conventional schooling being in those days considered out of the question, the Yorks wanted someone who would stimulate their daughters' minds without overburdening them with subject areas that would be little use to them in their royal life. 'Crawfie', as she was soon dubbed by her charges was, according to her own account, given a free rein when it came to educating the granddaughters of the King:

"No one ever had employers who interfered so little. I often had the feeling the Duke and Duchess, most happy in their own married life, were not over concerned with the higher education of their daughters. They wanted most for them a really happy childhood, with lots of pleasant memories stored up against the days that might come and, later, happy marriages."

Someone who was 'over concerned' about the education of the two princesses was their grandmother. Queen Mary asked Crawfie to send her a draft copy of the curriculum that the Yorks had approved. She was dismayed to see that while the mornings were filled with half hour lessons, the afternoons were given over to less academic pursuits such as singing and dancing.

The Queen insisted that more history, geography and bible reading should be included. "Her Majesty felt that genealogies, historical and dynastic, were very interesting to children" recalled the governess, "and, for these children, really important."

In Mary's eyes the girls needed to be constantly made aware of their heritage and the part the British Empire had played on the world's stage. To this end she wanted lessons to have a royal bias; so for example their knowledge of Geography should concentrate on India, the Dominions

Clockwise from top left – The princesses pose outside *Y Bwythn Bach* (the Little House) the cottage given to them by the people of Wales in 1932; the Silver Jubilee in 1935; wearing a coral necklace in 1927; a solemn Elizabeth in a horse drawn carriage with Margaret and their nanny 1933 and a photo of the four year old princess taken by her father as she poses among a group of Madonna Lillies

The wedding of Prince George to Princess Marina of Greece in 1934. George V stands next to the bride's mother Princess Nicholas of Greece (top left); Queen Mary stands next to Prince Nicholas (top right). Two of the bridesmaids sit at the front, eight year old Elizabeth (left) and Lady Mary Cambridge.

*Interspersed with lessons at 145 Piccadilly,
the future Queen had a walk-on part
at the major royal ceremonies of the 1930s.*

of Canada, Australia and New Zealand and all the other territories that George V was King-Emperor of.

Interspersed with lessons at 145 Piccadilly, the future Queen had a walk-on part at the major royal ceremonies of the 1930s. In November 1934, aged eight, she was bridesmaid at the Westminster Abbey wedding of her uncle Prince George, Duke of Kent, to the beautiful and stylish Princess Marina of Greece.

Lady Cynthia Colville, a Woman of the Bedchamber to Queen Mary, noted: "she played her part with dignity and sang froid."

The following year she attended her grandfather's Silver Jubilee thanksgiving service held at St Paul's Cathedral on 6 May 1935. Despite their four year age difference, the two girls were nearly always dressed identically at public events, and appeared in rosebud pink coats and hats for the Jubilee.

Inside St Paul's they sat on specially made stools, behind their grandparents' throne-like chairs. Later they appeared on the Buckingham Palace balcony and listened to the King's broadcast.

Like the current jubilee, the 1935 event was celebrated against a backdrop of economic gloom. Some critics had questioned the appropriateness of such a lavish spectacle in such stringent times, but the huge upsurge of affection for the well-loved monarch proved them wrong.

George was hugely touched: "I had no idea they felt that about me," he said afterwards. "I'm beginning to think they like me for myself."

Later that year both Elizabeth and Margaret were bridesmaids to the King's third son Prince Henry, Duke of Gloucester, who married Lady Alice Montagu-Douglas-Scott. This time the ceremony was held in the private chapel at Buckingham Palace due to the recent death of the bride's father.

In December 2001, Princess Alice celebrated her 100th birthday. A few days earlier she joined friends and family for a short ceremony outside her Kensington Palace home. They watched a military parade by the King's Own Scottish Borderers, of whom Princess Alice had been Colonel-in-Chief for more than sixty years. Sitting either side of her that day were her two royal bridesmaids. Poignantly it was to be the last public appearance of both Princess Alice and her niece Princess Margaret.

The year 1936 was to be one of the most eventful of the young Elizabeth's life. In January she was playing in the snow on the lawns of Sandringham House in Norfolk when her grandmother came out to tell her that the king was very ill indeed, and after lunch she went in to see him for what would be the last time.

The two princesses returned to Windsor and their governess was summoned back from her Christmas holiday to look after them. "Don't let all this depress them more than is absolutely necessary, Crawfie," the Duchess of York wrote. "They are so young."

The nine and a half year old Elizabeth was sensitive to the sombre atmosphere and whispered conversations between the adults at Royal Lodge and asked, "Oh Crawfie, ought we to play?"

The King died shortly before midnight on 20 January. The girls were considered too young to attend the elaborate state funeral, though Elizabeth was taken to see her grandfather's body lying in state in Westminster Hall.

Dressed in a black velvet coat and hat she watched mesmerised as her father and his three brothers stood guard over the late king's body in what became known as 'The Vigil of the Princes.'

It was a scene that she herself would authorise to be

repeated three quarters of a century later when her own three sons and her nephew, Viscount Linley, stood guard over the Queen Mother's body as it lay in state on the same site.

On her return she reported the scene to her governess, adding: "Uncle David was there and he never moved at all…. not even an eyelid."

Uncle David was by then King Edward VIII. For over 25 years he had been the darling of the empire, popular and charismatic and in tune with the modern world.

While his father had maintained the traditions and standards of the Victorian court, Edward was forward thinking and innovative. There was only one problem - at the age of 42 he was unmarried and, although the wider public had no knowledge of it, the only woman in his life was a twice-divorced American socialite called Wallis Simpson.

As with the death of the King, Elizabeth was shielded from the raw reality of the effect Edward's romance was having on her parents. The new king grew increasingly

determined to marry Wallis, and, when it became clear the British and Dominion parliaments were not prepared to back him, Edward decided to renounce the throne rather than the woman he loved.

Elizabeth only met Mrs Simpson once during her uncle's reign. Edward and Wallis drove to Royal Lodge to show the Yorks his new American station wagon. The princesses were brought in to meet them and Wallis later recalled: "They were both so blonde, so beautifully mannered, so brightly scrubbed that they might have stepped straight out of a picture book."

On Friday 11 December 1936 parliament ratified the instrument of abdication that Edward had signed the previous day. Bertie became king and decided to use the last of his four Christian names and to reign as George VI rather than King Albert.

Ten year old Elizabeth formerly became heir to the throne and it is said the family's new status really hit her when she was noticed a letter on the hall table addressed to 'Her Majesty the Queen' and said: "That's *Mummy* now isn't it?"

(Opposite) In his Abdication broadcast to the nation, Edward VIII said of his brother who was succeeding him as George VI: "He has one matchless blessing, enjoyed by so many of you, and not bestowed on me – a happy home with his wife and children." During his short reign of fifteen years the new king would find constant support from Queen Elizabeth and their children.

King George VI and Queen Elizabeth with their daughters Princess Elizabeth and Princess Margaret Rose after the Coronation of the Duke of York as King George VI. May 12, 1937.

Elizabeth and Margaret join their parents on the balcony of Buckingham Palace following the Coronation of George VI. Their formidable grandmother, Queen Mary, (centre) broke with tradition and attended the ceremony to give a show a family unity in the aftermath of the Abdication five months earlier. May 12, 1937.

On 17 February 1937 Elizabeth and her family moved into Buckingham Palace where, apart from the short period following her marriage until her accession, she has lived ever since.

The Coronation took place on 12 May: the date originally chosen for the crowning of Edward VIII.

By then Elizabeth was aged eleven and Margaret not quite seven. Once again the two girls were dressed identically. Their long white silver dresses were made of lace and adorned with small silver bows. They each had a full train of purple velvet trimmed with ermine and, at the King's request, wore specially commissioned lightweight coronets.

They rode to the Abbey in a carriage with Queen Mary and their great aunt, Queen Maud of Norway, and were cheered ecstatically. A machine placed on a rooftop in Whitehall recorded that whilst the coach carrying the King and Queen had registered cheers of 83 decibels from the crowd, the one carrying the princesses and their grandmother scored 85.

Elizabeth was now Heiress Presumptive (a variant of the usual title 'Heir Apparent' was used in case her mother, still only in her late 30s, produced a son). Surprisingly, given her change in status, her tutelage continued under Marion Crawford. The only change, in recognition of her future role, was the addition of lessons on British constitutional history under Sir Henry Marten the Vice-Provost of Eton College.

Used to teaching only roomfuls of adolescent boys, the slightly eccentric Marten nervously chewed the corner of his handkerchief, crunched lumps of sugar and addressed the princess as 'gentlemen.'

On 22 July 1939, during the last summer of peace before the Second World War, the princesses visited Dartmouth Naval College with their parents. An outbreak of both mumps and chicken pox at the college meant that not only were many of the cadets quarantined during the visit but the princesses were obliged to stay marooned in the house of the officer in charge, Sir Frederick Dalrymple-Hamilton. Marion Crawford records that the girls were playing croquet

on the lawns when they were joined by "a fair-haired boy, rather like a Viking, with a sharp face and piercing blue eyes." This was Prince Philip of Greece, who, like Elizabeth, was a great-great-grandchild of Queen Victoria.

The two had both attended the wedding of Prince George and Princess Marina in 1934 but had no recollection of seeing each other. According to nearly every biography of the Queen and Prince Philip, Dartmouth was their first proper meeting and the first time they took notice of each other.

Philip was eighteen – five years older than Elizabeth and nine years older than Margaret – and was clearly bored with having to entertain his two distant cousins. Instead he suggested they go outside to the tennis court "and have some real fun jumping the nets." According to Crawfie a besotted Lilibet "never took her eyes off him the whole time."

The princesses were staying at Balmoral Castle, the private royal residence in Aberdeenshire, when war was declared on 3 September 1939. Their parents had returned to London and decided it was best for the girls to stay in

Scotland with Crawfie for the foreseeable future.

With no invasion imminent by Christmas the girls joined the King and Queen at Sandringham for the festivities. It was then decided that they should spend the rest of the war at Windsor Castle. Officially the princesses were said to be staying 'somewhere in the country,' and the exact location was never revealed until after hostilities ceased in 1945.

The children of many aristocratic families were sent to Canada or America for the duration and pointedly keeping the princesses in Britain was regarded as robustly defiant. Their mother, Queen Elizabeth, memorably declared: "The children won't leave without me; I won't leave without the King; and the King will never leave."

Crawfie, Alah and Bobo stayed with the princesses at Windsor. In an interview in 1995, to mark the fiftieth anniversary of the end of the war, Princess Margaret recalls that the castle was surrounded "by rather flimsy barbed wire, which wouldn't have kept the Germans out, but certainly kept us in."

(Above) Prince Philip of Greece escorts the royal party to the wedding of the Hon. Patricia Mountbatten to Captain Lord Brabourne at Romsey Abbey, Hampshire in 1946. The two princesses, wearing mink coats and carrying flowers, were bridesmaids. By now Elizabeth and Philip were doing little to hide their relationship and the press began to speculate that about the royal romance.

(Left) Elizabeth, seen here with Margaret, made her first radio broadcast in 1940, aged 14, to the children of the empire.

(Opposite) By the end of the war Elizabeth had joined the ATS and wore her uniform as she posed with her parents, sister and the architect of victory, Winston Churchill, on the balcony of Buckingham Palace on VE Day. May 1945.

A radiant Elizabeth is supported by Philip as they leave
Westminster Abbey following their wedding service.
The princess had fought hard to convince her parents that
Philip, her first real boyfriend, was the man she wanted to
spend the rest of her life with. November 20, 1947.

On 13 October 1940, the 14 year old Elizabeth made her first radio broadcast, in which she sent her best wishes to the children who had been evacuated from Britain to Canada and elsewhere. The short address featured, appropriately enough, on *Children's Hour* and at the end of it she asked ten-year-old Margaret to join her to say "Goodnight" to their listeners.

A useful distraction during the war years was the annual pantomimes the girls staged with members of the household and estate workers in the Waterloo Chamber. Princess Elizabeth was usually the Principal Boy to her sister's heroine in *Cinderella*, *The Sleeping Beauty*, *Aladdin* and *Old Mother Red Riding Boots*.

Elizabeth had wanted to play her part in the war effort and her wish was finally granted early in 1945 when she became No 230873 Second Subaltern HRH Princess Elizabeth in the Auxiliary Territorial Service (ATS). She learned how to strip and service an engine as well as the basics of vehicle maintenance.

When the European war ended in May 1945, Elizabeth wore her ATS uniform as she joined Margaret and their parents alongside Prime Minister, Winston Churchill, on the balcony of Buckingham Palace on VE Day. Later in the day the two girls, along with a party of friends, joined revellers in The Mall. The future Queen knocked off a policeman's helmet and later danced a conga through the Ritz Hotel before shouting, "We Want the King" outside the palace railings.

With the cessation of hostilities, Elizabeth began to take on more royal engagements, quite often accompanying her parents, but increasingly on her own as well.

She also began to become more attached to Philip who had been away for the six years of war serving with the royal navy. He had been mentioned in dispatches following the Battle of Matapan and had witnessed the Japanese surrender in Tokyo Bay in August 1945.

The King and Queen were initially alarmed that their eldest daughter was falling headlong in love at the tender age of twenty. They arranged parties and invited a whole series of eligible aristocrats to dance and chat to Elizabeth.

Queen Mary dubbed them 'the bodyguard' and realized her son and his wife were wasting their time. Speaking to her lady-in-waiting about the situation she said her granddaughter "would always know her own mind. There's something very steadfast and determined in her."

For the princess there was an added problem. In February 1947 she and Margaret were committed to joining the King and Queen on a major tour of South Africa that would last until mid May.

The mammoth 23,000 mile progress was exhausting and although the princess kept in regular touch with Philip by letter and telephone, the strain on her was noticeable and at times she looked tired and subdued.

On 21 April, in the final stages of the tour, Elizabeth celebrated her 21st birthday whilst in Cape Town. It was from here that she made one of her most memorable broadcasts during which she pledged her life to serve the peoples of the Empire.

"I declare before you," she vowed, "that my whole life, whether it be long or short, shall be devoted to your service and the service of our great Imperial Commonwealth to which we all belong."

Two months after Elizabeth's return to Britain, King George gave his blessing to his daughter's engagement and on 10th July 1947 it was formerly announced that "with the greatest pleasure" the King and Queen announced "the betrothal of their dearly beloved daughter."

The ceremony at Westminster Abbey was billed as 'an austerity wedding.' Having said that it was also one of the largest gatherings of reigning and exiled European royalty of the century and the bride was inundated with presents from people from all walks of life – 1,500 gifts were listed in the official catalogue.

Winston Churchill called the wedding "a flash of colour on the hard road we have to travel." Much of the colour was provided by the Household Cavalry escort making one of its first post-war ceremonial appearances.

Elizabeth looked every inch the radiant bride in her Norman Hartnell ivory duchesse satin wedding gown inspired by Botticelli's painting *Primavera*. Philip, newly created Duke of Edinburgh, wore his naval uniform and the badge and sash of the Order of the Garter, which the King had bestowed on him shortly before the wedding.

Afterwards the couple left for their honeymoon destination of Broadlands, the Hampshire home of Philip's uncle, Lord Mountbatten.

It was while they were there that Elizabeth received a touching letter from her father. The King wrote: "I was so proud of you and thrilled at having you so close to me on our long walk in Westminster Abbey, but when I handed your hand to the Archbishop, I felt I had lost something very precious. You were so calm and composed during the Service and said your words with such conviction, that I knew everything was all right."

Just under a year later the Princess gave birth to her first child, a 7lb 6oz son, on Sunday, 14 November 1948.

The baby was born at Buckingham Palace where a crowd of 3,000 onlookers gathered to be the first to hear the news that Elizabeth was "safely delivered of a son at 9:14pm." 81-year-old Queen Mary was cheered as she drove the short distance from Marlborough House to inspect her new great grandson and in Trafalgar Square the fountains changed to 'blue for a boy.'

The latest addition to the royal family was christened Charles Philip Arthur George in a short ceremony at Buckingham Palace on 15 December. The new mother wrote to tell a friend that the baby's hands "are rather large but fine with long fingers – quite unlike mine and certainly unlike his father's. It will be interesting to see what they become. I still find it difficult to believe I have a baby of my own."

In 1949 the Edinburghs moved into Clarence House. Elizabeth resumed her royal duties and Philip returned to naval duties, joining HMS Chequers, part of the Mediterranean fleet. The princess flew out to Malta to join him for Christmas 1949, the first of two lengthy stays on the island and the only time in her life she was free from her official life and duties.

Here the princess lived the life of an officer's wife attending parties and polo matches, enjoying swimming and dancing, and going on shopping trips and visits to the hairdresser.

In between her two visits to Malta, Elizabeth returned home for the birth of Princess Anne, on 15 August 1950, at Clarence House.

In October 1951 Elizabeth and Philip were away from home for 35 days carrying out a successful tour of Canada and the United States. They crossed the North American continent twice, covering 10,000 miles in Canada alone.

"We've just had a visit from a lovely young lady and her personable husband," wrote US President Harry S Truman to the King, adding: "they went to the hearts of all the citizens of the United States."

George VI was proud of his daughter and son-in-law and on their return he appointed them members of the Privy Council, on 4 December 1951.

As her father's health declined, Elizabeth was increasingly taking on more duties. In June 1951 she deputised for him at the Trooping the Colour ceremony, and the following month Philip left the navy on indefinite leave to resume his royal engagements in Britain.

Late in September the King had his left lung removed during an operation performed by his surgeons at Buckingham Palace.

The King rallied and by the end of January 1952 when his doctors examined him at Sandringham they expressed themselves well satisfied with his progress.

Two days later he travelled to London airport with the Queen and Princess Margaret to wave goodbye to Elizabeth and Philip as they embarked on a tour of East Africa, Australia and New Zealand.

It was noted that the King braved the cold to watch the aircraft steadily rise into the clouds until it was a tiny dot on the horizon.

The loving father and his dutiful daughter would never see each other again.

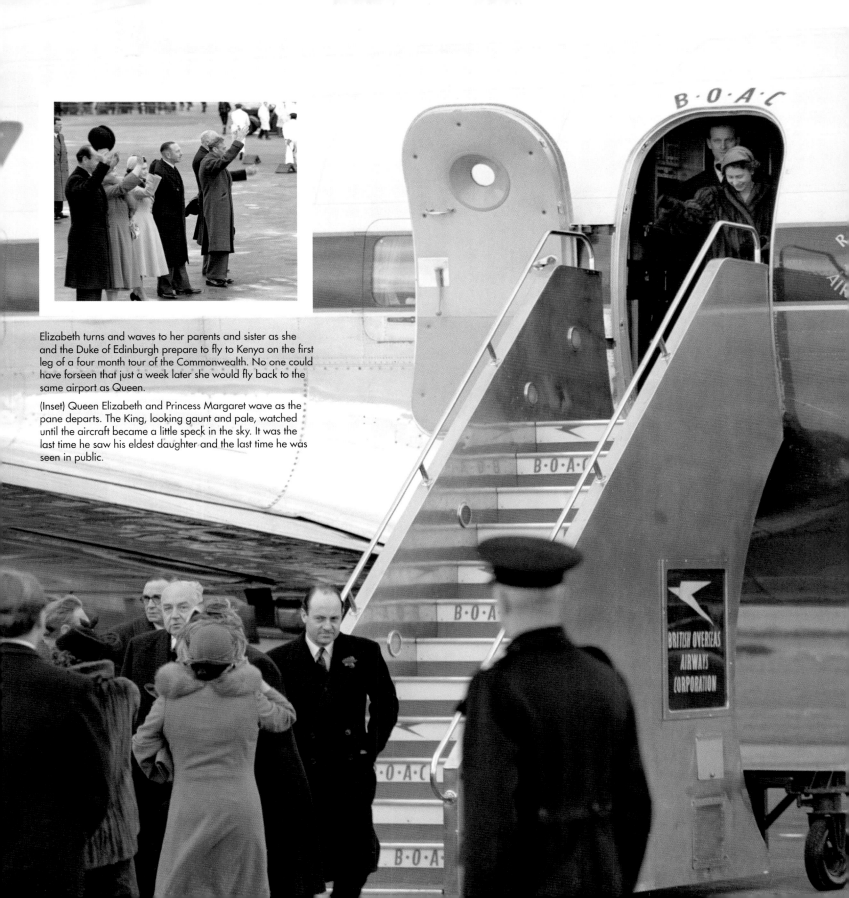

Elizabeth turns and waves to her parents and sister as she and the Duke of Edinburgh prepare to fly to Kenya on the first leg of a four month tour of the Commonwealth. No one could have forseen that just a week later she would fly back to the same airport as Queen.

(Inset) Queen Elizabeth and Princess Margaret wave as the pane departs. The King, looking gaunt and pale, watched until the aircraft became a little speck in the sky. It was the last time he saw his eldest daughter and the last time he was seen in public.

Through his marriage to Queen Elizabeth and the love of their two daughters, George VI found much of the security that had been missing during his own unhappy childhood. He referred to their family as "we four" and said of his daughters that Elizabeth was his pride and Margaret his joy.

Family Life

*A happy family life is vital to the Queen.
It offers reassuring support and allows her to cope
with the stresses and strains of her public duties.*

Last Christmas Eve we saw how Elizabeth's children rallied round when Prince Philip was taken ill and rushed to Papworth Hospital for heart surgery. Princes Andrew and Edward and Princess Anne flew with their mother by helicopter from Sandringham to see the Duke. Prince Charles and Camilla, arrived separately by car the same afternoon.

The following day, while the Queen was hosting the festivities in Norfolk, her six eldest grandchildren drove to the hospital to ensure Philip had visitors and to report back with the latest news.

By coincidence family was the theme of the pre-recorded Christmas Broadcast. The Queen said: "The importance of family has, of course, come home to Prince Philip and me personally this year with the marriages of two of our grandchildren, each in their own way a celebration of the God-given love that binds a family together."

This "God-given love" was shown to her at an early age by her parents, the Duke and Duchess of York. The Duke had suffered a miserable childhood and was determined to ensure that his two daughters would be very much loved.

In his Abdication Speech, Elizabeth's uncle, Edward VIII, sounded envious of the Yorks' home life. Referring to his brother, Edward said: "He has one matchless blessing, enjoyed by so many of you, and not bestowed on me - a happy home with his wife and children".

Following her father's death in 1952 Elizabeth remained close to both her mother and sister. The three spoke to each other by telephone most days and a courtier once said: "upset one of them and you upset them all."

Prince Philip's own childhood was disrupted when his mother was diagnosed with schizophrenia and sent to live in a series of sanatoria. For five years, during his teens, Philip neither saw nor heard from her. At the same time his father left for Monte Carlo where he set up home with his mistress.

Philip therefore found stability with the unchanging routine of life with the Royal Family. He found a soulmate in the Queen and they have much in common, from a sense of humour and gift of mimicry to a love of horses and the outdoors.

It was difficult for them to spend the time they would have liked with their eldest two children, due to the pressure of their new lives as monarch and consort, but, a decade on, it was easier the second time round with Andrew and Edward.

He found a soulmate with the Queen and they have much in common from a sense of humour and gift of mimicry to a love of horses and the outdoors.

While the Queen is head of state, Philip is very much head of the family and takes charge at family get-togethers such as Christmas at Sandringham and summers at Balmoral.

In that same Christmas Broadcast of 2011, the Queen said: "We've seen that it's in hardship that we often find strength from our families." At no time in her life was this more evident than in the 1990s during her 'Annus Horribilis' of 1992 and the death of Diana five years later. She was devastated by the divorces of three of her children but, with the help and advice of Philip and her mother and sister, was able to get through this and similar crises.

These days she is supported by "my young friends", as she refers to her grandchildren. William, Harry, Beatrice and Zara have all said in interviews how much they love and admire the Queen.

This special year, Elizabeth's four children and princes William and Harry will represent the Queen on Jubilee tours around nearly every part of the Commonwealth. They will also be by her side in St Paul's Cathedral for the Thanksgiving Service in June, a show of unity for their sovereign, but more importantly their mother and grandmother.

(Clockwise from the top) During her fifty year widowhood, Queen Elizabeth, known affectionately to the nation as the 'Queen Mum', continued to support her two daughters. The three women usually spoke to each other every day by telephone. Here they appear outside Clarence House on the Queen Mother's 93rd birthday.

(Bottom right) The Queen is proud of the hard work her grandsons William and Harry have put into developing their careers and realises the future of the monarchy is safe in their capable hands. Trooping the Colour June 2008.

(Bottom Left) While the Queen is head of the nation, Prince Philip is very much head of the family and is involved in the running of the royal estates including this one, Balmoral Castle, where they are shown posing for a Silver Wedding photo in 1972.

Queen Elizabeth II wearing the Imperial Crown, carries the symbols of authority, the orb and the sceptre, as she leaves Westminster Abbey. June 2, 1953.

A New Elizabethan Age

1952 – 1962

King George VI died peacefully in his sleep in the early hours of 6 February 1952. His eldest daughter succeeded to the throne as Queen Elizabeth II. She was only 25.

A New Elizabethan Age

Elizabeth II became Queen on 6 February 1952. Her accession was unusual for two reasons. Firstly she was the first monarch for almost 250 years to be out of the country when she became monarch. Secondly, we have no idea of the exact time she became Queen.

The King retired to bed at Sandringham on Tuesday 5th after listening to a news bulletin mentioning Elizabeth's tour. A watchman heard him adjust the latch on his bedroom window at about midnight. Sometime between then and 7:30am when valet James McDonald entered his room with a cup of tea, George VI died of a coronary thrombosis.

At the time Elizabeth and Philip were on the first leg of their extensive tour of East Africa, Australia and New Zealand. On the night of her accession she was staying at Treetops, a three-bedroomed hotel, built into a giant fig tree. It was sited near to a watering hole where wildlife came to drink, and the delighted princess shot photo after photo of them. At one point she saw a waterbuck killed in a fight at the pool. She would recall her stay as "one of the most wonderful experiences" she had known.

The next morning, as she descended the rickety ladder and walked back through the jungle trail she was, without knowing it, already Queen of the United Kingdom and its Commonwealth.

It took about four hours for the news to reach the royal party and to be confirmed.

While Elizabeth and Philip were resting at Sagana Lodge, loaned to them as a wedding present by the people of Kenya in 1947, her Private Secretary, Martin Charteris went over to the Outspan Hotel where the press were staying. A local journalist asked him to confirm a Reuters report that the King had died.

Charteris hurriedly contacted Mike Parker, Philip's Private Secretary, who managed to telephone through to London to get official confirmation from the palace. Finally at 2:45pm local time, 11:45am back in London, Parker told the Duke who, on the pretext of showing Elizabeth the fish in the garden pond, took her outside and walked round and round the grounds, slowly breaking the awful news to her.

Parker later recalled that the Duke appeared more devastated by what had happened than his wife: "He looked as if you'd dropped half the world on him. I never felt so sorry for anyone in my life." Philip was after all only 30 and the new Queen a mere 25.

Preparations now had to be hastily made for the royal party to return to the UK. Before that Charteris had one essential administrative duty to perform and that was to ask the new Queen what name she wished to be known by – after all Victoria and Edward VII had chosen their second names and George VI had chosen his fourth. Elizabeth replied, "oh, my own name – what else?"

The royal party then had to fly some 4,000 miles back to the United Kingdom via Uganda and Libya. She finally reached London airport at 4pm on the 7th. There to greet her on the tarmac was her uncle, the Duke of Gloucester, her Prime Minister Winston Churchill and the Leader of the Opposition Clement Attlee.

Elizabeth drove to her London home Clarence House rather than Buckingham Palace. It was a lonely

The King retired to bed at Sandringham on Tuesday 5th. He passed away sometime between midnight and 7:30am. George VI died of a coronary thrombosis.

Elizabeth II sets foot on British soil for the first time as Queen. Wearing a black coat over a dark green dress, the 25 year old monarch descends the steps of the BOAC Argonaut Atlanta. Waiting to meet her are (Left to Right) Lord Woolton, President of the Privy Council; Anthony Eden, Foreign Secretary, Clement Attlee, Leader of the Opposition Party and Winston Churchill, the Prime Minister. London Airport, February 7, 1952.

(Left) Like characters from a Greek Tragedy three generations of British queens mourn their husband, father and son. Dominating the scene is the indomitable figure of Queen Mary, aged 84, who lost three of her sons during her lifetime. The widowed Queen Elizabeth stands to the right while the young Elizabeth II seems to be overawed by the scene. They stand at the door of Westminster Hall awaiting the coffin of George VI before its Lying in State. February 11, 1952.

(Bottom Right) The heavily veiled figure of Elizabeth II shakes hands with the Dean of Windsor, the Rt. Rev. Eric Knightley Chetwode Hamilton, after the funeral service for her father, the late King George VI, at St. George's Chapel, Windsor. In the background Prince Philip bends to kiss the hand of his widowed mother in law.

homecoming as her mother and sister were still at Sandringham with Charles and Anne. It was left to the new Queen's grandmother, 84-year-old Queen Mary to represent the family. Before driving the short distance from nearby Marlborough House she told a lady–in-waiting: "Her old grannie must be the first to kiss her hand."

Before paying her respects to her father and reuniting with her widowed mother and children, Elizabeth II had first to begin her official life. The morning following her return she met with the accession council at St James's Palace. She told the assembled politicians that she aimed to continue her father's work: "I pray that God will help me to discharge worthily the heavy task that has been laid upon me so early in my life."

Only then, after carrying out the duties of a monarch, could she mourn as a daughter and travel to Sandringham to be reunited with her family and to prepare for her father's funeral.

Elizabeth and Philip had only moved into the newly refurbished Clarence House in 1949. They very much hoped that they could continue to live there and to use the palace more or less as an office. Unfortunately they reckoned with out the 'old guard' who would heavily influence the young Queen during the early years of her reign. Sir Alan Lascelles, George VI's Private Secretary, who now served the new Queen in the same capacity, and other senior courtiers, insisted the couple had to be based at Buckingham Palace, one of the main symbols of the monarchy. He also had the backing of Churchill who said simply: "To the Palace they must go."

Philip soon realised, that as a mere consort, he had no right or power to combat the palace mandarins. Another blow to his confidence came just less than two months after the accession. His uncle Earl Mountbatten was overheard boasting at a house party that the house of Mountbatten now reigned. Prince Ernst August of Hanover, a grandson of Kaiser Wilhelm II, was a fellow guest and reported the conversation to Queen Mary. It was her husband, King George V, who had named his dynasty the House of Windsor in 1917 and fearing Mountbatten was about

The Duke of Edinburgh embraces the Queen after paying homage to her during her Coronation in Westminster Abbey.

to jeopardise this she immediately sent for Jock Colville, Churchill's Private Secretary.

Again Churchill and the palace old guard united. They backed Queen Mary and in April Elizabeth II signed an order in council that stated: "That I and My children shall be styled and known as the House of Windsor." Philip memorably protested: "I am nothing but a bloody amoeba. I am the only man in the country not allowed to give his name to his own children."

Queen Mary herself survived her son by only 14 months. She died on 24 March 1953. Realising that she would not live to see the Coronation of her granddaughter on 2 June she gave orders that court mourning for her passing should not interfere with preparations for the day.

It was partly to mollify Prince Philip, who felt increasingly that he was being sidelined by his wife's officials, that Elizabeth appointed him Chairman of the newly founded Coronation Commission.

He was one of the ones in favour of televising the Coronation live. The Queen had at first been reluctant

fearing the added strain this would add to an already nerve-wracking day. Finally, quite late on in the proceedings, she gave into pressure from all sides – especially the media – and agree to a live broadcast. Millions of her subjects gained a ringside seat in this most ancient of ceremonies and the sales of televisions soared in the run-up to the day.

Unlike Queen Mary or Queen Elizabeth the Queen Mother, male consorts, such as Prince Philip are not crowned. Instead he remained an onlooker like the rest of the royal family. His only part in the ceremony was when he knelt before her and promised to become her "liege man of life and limb, and of earthly worship... So help me God."

For each of her jubilees, including the present one, the Queen and Duke have repeated the pattern they began in 1953. That summer they undertook a tour of the UK to meet her people. They visited Scotland where the Honours of Scotland – the Scottish Crown Jewels were proffered to her in Edinburgh. She also went to Northern Ireland.

Later in the year the Queen and Duke set off on what would be the longest tour of her reign. They were away from Britain for five and a half months on a massive imperial progress round the Commonwealth.

They would visit places as diverse as Bermuda, Jamaica, Fiji. Tonga, the Coco Islands, Aden, Uganda, Malta and Gibraltar. They also spent three months in Australia and New Zealand and ten days in Ceylon, and the Queen wore her Coronation dress to open parliament in each of these countries. She would wear it once more in 1957 when she also opened parliament in Canada.

The Queen and Duke travelled 44,000 miles by air, sea and land on the 1953-4 tour, and it was estimated that, in Australia, three quarters of the population turned out to catch a glimpse – mostly a very distant one – of their monarch. For the only time in her life, Elizabeth spent Christmas outside the UK, and made her annual broadcast live from Auckland, New Zealand. On her arrival in that country the Maoris hailed her as 'The Rare White Heron of the Single Flight.'

On their return journey the royal couple were reunited with Prince Charles and Princess Anne in Malta.

Elizabeth looks tense as she makes her Christmas broadcast to the peoples of the Commonwealth from Government House, Auckland, New Zealand. She was on a six month post Coronation tour and it was the first and only time she spent the festive season abroad. December 25, 1953.

(Opposite) The newly crowned monarch appears on the Balcony of Buckingham Palace following her Coronation. June 2, 1953.

(Left) At the start of her six month Commonwealth tour, the Queen, flanked by Sir Alexander Hood, Governor of Bermuda, (left), and the Duke of Edinburgh, receives a speech of welcome from Mayor E. R. Williams at Hamilton, Bermuda. November 24, 1953.

(Below) Four weeks later the Queen had reached Tonga and was reunited with Queen Salote who had endeared herself during Elizabeth's Coronation procession by refusing to have her carriage covered despite the heavy rain.

(Opposite) Not always seeing eye to eye. The Queen and Princess Margaret, right, attend the West Norfolk hunt point-to-point races at Sporle, England. April 30, 1955.

LONG LIVE THE QUEEN

The children had sailed to meet their mother on the new Royal Yacht *Britannia*, which Elizabeth had launched in April 1953 on Clydeside. The interior was designed by Hugh Casson with input from both Elizabeth and Philip. Casson later recalled: "The overall idea was to give the impression of a country house at sea." He recalled: "The Queen is a meticulous observer with very strong views on everything from the door-handles to the shape of the lampshades."

While the Queen was preoccupied with her new life as queen and mother, her sister Princess Margaret found it hard to adjust to her new role. She was no longer the daughter of a sovereign, living at Buckingham Palace. She now moved in with her widowed mother at Clarence House and her life, outside the routine of royal engagements, was directionless.

More worryingly for her family Margaret had fallen in love with her father's equerry, Peter Townsend, who continued to serve the Queen Mother as comptroller after the King's death.

On the day of the Coronation, an eagle-eyed journalist noticed Princess Margaret brush a fleck of dust from Townsend's uniform as the royal party waited to leave the service. It was an obviously intimate gesture.

Shortly before the Coronation, Margaret told her mother and sister that she was in love and wanted to marry. The Queen Mother, once dubbed 'the imperial ostrich' for her ability to ignore distasteful matters, did nothing. The young Queen asked her sister to put matters on hold: "Under the circumstances," she said, "it isn't unreasonable for me to ask you to wait a year."

The news story eventually broke in mid-June when the *People* newspaper ran a front-page story revealing all the speculation printed by its foreign counterparts. Meanwhile, hoping that distance might lessen the couple's infatuation, the palace arranged for Townsend to have a posting in Brussels for two years as an air attaché. Margaret, who was on a tour of Rhodesia with her mother at the time, was furious that she wasn't even allowed to say goodbye.

The romance died down but the couple kept in touch.

While the Queen was preoccupied with her new life as queen and mother, her sister Princess Margaret, found it hard to adjust to her new role.

Two years later the flames were fanned again when Townsend returned from Belgium in the autumn of 1955. By then Margaret had reached 25. Under the terms of the 1772 Royal Marriages Act, she would be free to marry the divorced Townsend without the consent of the Queen, providing she could secure the approval of parliament. In doing so she would lose her Civil List payment and her position as third in line to the throne.

It was a similar dilemma to the one faced by her uncle, King Edward VIII, a generation earlier. This time, however, duty came before personal fulfilment. On 31 October 1955, Margaret announced that: "Mindful of the church's teaching that Christian marriage is indissoluble, and conscious of my duty to the Commonwealth, I have resolved to put these considerations before others." The princess gave up the man she loved rather than face a life of exile and ostracism.

It was the Queen's own private life that came under scrutiny the following year.

Prince Philip still found it intolerable dealing with the palace old guard, who routinely consulted the Queen on nearly every issue but left the Duke very much to his own devices.

In October 1956, Philip set off on a solo four-month tour that took him to Australia, New Zealand, Ceylon, the Gambia, Antarctica and the Falkland Islands. Biographers have suggested this was a sign that the marriage was in trouble and that the Duke had decided enough was enough. Palace officials insist, even to this day, that the purpose of the tour was only for Philip to open the Melbourne Olympic Games and to visit the smaller dependent territories that were not included in the earlier Commonwealth tour.

Nonetheless, in retrospect, it is hard not to conclude that there was something amiss. When the Queen and Duke were reunited in Portugal in February 1957 the Duke emerged from his aeroplane wearing a tie with love hearts on it, which made headlines in the following day's newspapers. While he was away he had grown a beard. When his wife appeared on board his jet she and her lady-in-waiting were both wearing false beards. It was the perfect icebreaker.

The same month the Queen announced that her husband was to be granted the title of Prince of the United Kingdom, something that had been overlooked when he was created Duke of Edinburgh on the eve of his wedding.

While the Duke was overseas, the Queen was involved with the greatest political crisis of her reign so far. Churchill had tendered his resignation in April 1955 at the age of eighty. In January 1957 his successor, Anthony Eden, saw the Queen at Sandringham to tell her his doctors had advised him also to step down as premier. Elizabeth now had to choose a leader from the Conservative party that was still split over Britain's aborted intervention in the Suez crisis the previous year.

Two candidates emerged as a potential leader: 'Rab' Butler, who had deputised for the ailing Eden, and Harold Macmillan, the Chancellor of the Exchequer. Although Butler was regarded by many as the favourite, the Conservatives in those days had no mechanism for electing a leader. Instead two peers took informal soundings within the government whilst Edward Heath, the chief whip, did the same with the other Tory MPs.

One of the peers, Lord Salisbury, went to see the Queen on 10 January to tell her that most government ministers and MPs backed Macmillan. The Queen also sought advice from

The Queen announced that her husband was to be granted the title of Prince of the United Kingdom, something that had been overlooked when he was created Duke of Edinburgh on the eve of his wedding.

Queen Elizabeth II is greeted by Lady Churchill and Sir Winston Churchill, as she arrives for a dinner party at No. 10 Downing Street. Churchill was the first of Elizabeth's twelve Prime Ministers to date and it was seen as a great honour that she should dine with him to mark his retirement. April 5, 1955.

The Queen's decision to televise her Christmas Broadcast proved popular and brought her closer to her subjects. Here Mrs Sidney Smart of London watches this first telecast with daughters Sandra aged four and Barbara, 15. December 25, 1957.

(Opposite) In the line of duty. Elizabeth listens as Prime Minister Harold Macmillan making his speech at the opening of the 46th Inter-Parliamentary Conference in Westminster Hall, London. September 1957.

Saturday Evening Post.

Around the same time, one of the original 'Angry Young Men,' the playwright John Osborne, wrote in *The Times*: "My objection to the Royal Family is that it is dead: it is a gold filling in a mouth full of decay."

The attacks hit home. Previous generations of royalty might have ignored them, but these were new times. Rock 'n roll was sweeping in from America and the youth culture of late 50s Britain wasn't going to worry about deference or the monarchy.

Things slowly changed at the palace. The archaic tradition of presentations at court, where the ruling classes could parade their daughters in front of the monarch, was abolished the following year. Decades later, Princess Margaret gave her own interpretation, "we had to stop it" she said, "because every tart in London was getting in."

The palace was also hosting informal lunch parties in which the Queen got to meet people from all walks of life, though to be fair this initiative came about before Altrincham et al had vented their criticisms.

Television also played its part in bringing the monarch into closer contact with her subjects when the Queen's Christmas Broadcast was broadcast on TV for the first time in 1957. It proved a popular move and the following autumn the State Opening of Parliament was also televised for the first time.

Mindful of her own limited education, the Queen was very much influenced by Prince Philip when it came to the schooling of Charles and Anne. The Duke decided his son should follow in his footsteps and duly enrolled him as a boarder at Cheam Preparatory in September of 1957. The move made history, since Charles became the first royal heir to be educated outside palace walls.

The following July Charles was called to the headmaster's study to watch the closing ceremony of the 1958 Commonwealth Games at Cardiff Arms Park. The Queen had been due to attend but was confined to bed with sinusitis. Instead the Duke of Edinburgh was present while a taped-recorded message from Elizabeth was played to the 36,000-strong crowd.

Sir Winston Churchill, who had retired two years earlier, and he too backed the findings, so Elizabeth sent for Macmillan at 2pm the same day and asked him to form a government.

Just five years into the new reign there was a personal attack on the Queen and her advisers. In the edition of the *National and English Review* published on 31 August 1957, its editor, Lord Altrincham, criticised the way the palace was running things, The Queen, he wrote, came over as "a priggish schoolgirl, captain of the hockey team," who, he went on to say, "is unable to string a few sentences together without a written text." Altrincham went on to dismiss courtiers as "tweedy" and "a tight little enclave of English ladies and gentlemen."

The story rapidly became front-page news. Altrincham was slapped across the face by an outraged middle-aged man as he left a television studio and the Queen's cousin, the Earl of Strathmore announced: "Altrincham should be shot!"

Others joined in the criticism. Journalist Malcolm Muggeridge described the royal family as "a soap opera, a sort of substitute or ersatz religion" in an article in the

The Queen said the Games "have made this a memorable year for the principality." Then to everyone's surprise she announced: "I have decided to mark it further by an act which will, I hope, give as much pleasure to all Welshmen as it does to me. I intend to make my son Charles, Prince of Wales today."

The rest of her words were drowned out by cheers as she promised: "when he is grown up, I will present him to you at Caernarvon."

During the 1950s the Queen and Duke made several major overseas tours, though none of them were to be as lengthy as that first Commonwealth tour.

In 1956 the couple toured Nigeria, arriving on 28 January to a tremendous welcome.

Today this tour is best remembered for the Queen's visit to a leper colony, the 1950s equivalent of Princess Diana's involvement with AIDs charities thirty years later.

Local drums beat out the message 'Our mother is coming!' as the royal party arrived. The Queen and Duke agreed to adopt a leper child financially, to the delight of

the colony's supervisor. He said: "the visit will do more to conquer man's fear and hate of the disease than any other single act I can think of."

Then, as now, the royal couple also hosted one or more incoming State Visits a year. The first one was in June 1954 when King Gustaf VI of Sweden arrived for a four-day tour. This was also a family occasion since Gustaf's wife, Queen Louise, was Prince Philip's maternal aunt.

The Queen's first overseas State Visit was another family occasion. In June 1955, Elizabeth and Philip arrived in Oslo aboard *Britannia* for a three-day visit hosted by King Haakon VII, Elizabeth's great uncle. Haakon was born Carl of Denmark in 1872, he was a son-in-law of the Queen's great grandfather Edward VII, and was also a nephew of Queen Alexandra. In 1896 he had married his cousin Princess Maud of Wales in the chapel at Buckingham Palace.

The Queen has met all US presidents since Harry Truman, apart from Lyndon Johnson. In October 1957 she paid her first visit to the USA as monarch and attended

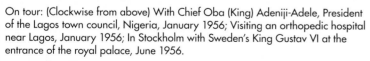

On tour: (Clockwise from above) With Chief Oba (King) Adeniji-Adele, President of the Lagos town council, Nigeria, January 1956; Visiting an orthopedic hospital near Lagos, January 1956; In Stockholm with Sweden's King Gustav VI at the entrance of the royal palace, June 1956.

(Opposite) Walking with US President Eisenhower past the Guard of Honour at Washington National Airport. October 17, 1957.

Elizabeth II, Queen of Canada, addresses the parliament in Ottawa wearing her Coronation gown, during her first tour as Queen. October 1957.

(Opposite) Two years later she is seen disembarking from her aircraft in London following her second Canadian tour. Newspapers voiced concern over her health after the 45-day tour, little realising that she was pregnant with her third child.

a banquet at the White House hosted by Dwight D Eisenhower. During the same visit she addressed the United Nations general assembly, an honour she would repeat exactly half a century later in 2007.

The last major tour of the decade was to Canada in June and July of 1959. During her gruelling 45-day stay she opened the St Lawrence Seaway in the presence of Eisenhower and the Canadian Prime Minister, John Diefenbaker.

Unusually the Queen pulled out of some of her engagements. Unknown to all but a few members of the royal party, the thirty-three-year old Elizabeth was in the early stages of her third pregnancy and understandably found the constant humidity a trial.

News of the Queen's condition was released on her return. During the autumn months Elizabeth withdrew from public life, as was customary for royal ladies in those days. As the 1950s ended, she and her family were at Sandringham House where they saw in the New Year, and looked forward to a new decade and, more importantly, a

new addition to the family.

Prince Andrew was born on 19 February 1960 and made history as the first child of a monarch to be born at Buckingham palace since Queen Victoria's child, Princess Beatrice in 1857.

Elizabeth had wanted a second family for some time. She was now 33 and had been Queen for eight years. She had relaxed into the role of monarch and could to a certain extent bring her personal life to the fore. This time round she was far more hands on, relishing nanny Mabel Anderson's night off so she could bath the baby prince and put him to bed herself. She taught him the alphabet and would often push him in his pram around the palace grounds.

Just over a week before the birth, the Queen made a significant announcement. On 8 February she declared her 'Will and Pleasure' that her descendant be called Mountbatten-Windsor. While she and her children would continue to be known as the House of Windsor, this new change would enable those of her descendants not entitled

Margaret's wedding was fixed for 6 May 1960. Foreign royals, dismayed at the princess marrying 'trade' stayed away in droves and the only significant presence was that of Queen Ingrid of Denmark

to be called his or her royal highness to adopt the new name.

In a separate statement from the palace, a spokesman said: "The Queen has always wanted, without changing the name of the royal house established by her grandfather, to associate the name of her husband with her own and his descendants."

On a more personal level it recognised the part Prince Philip was playing in her life as well as the life of the monarchy. He never wanted the Prince Consort title that Victoria had bestowed on Albert, but the fact his family name would live on was undoubtedly pleasing to him. Lady Louise Windsor, daughter of Prince Edward, was the first member of the family to be given the new surname, although Princess Anne, who officially doesn't need to use anything other than her Christian name, signed herself Mountbatten-Windsor on her wedding certificate in 1973.

February 1960 was proving to be an eventful month. The week after Andrew's birth it was announced that Princess Margaret would marry society photographer Antony Armstrong-Jones. Prime Minister Harold Macmillan recalled arriving at Sandringham the previous Christmas to be greeted by the blustering figure of the Queen's Uncle Henry, Duke of Gloucester, saying "Thank heavens you've come, Prime Minister. The Queen's in a terrible state; there's a fellow called Jones in the billiard room wants to marry her sister, and Prince Philip's in the library wanting to change the family name to Mountbatten!"

Margaret's wedding was fixed for 6 May 1960. Foreign royals, dismayed at the princess marrying 'trade', stayed away in droves and the only significant presence was that of Queen Ingrid of Denmark, the bride's godmother. Even members of the British royal family were unenthusiastic. When Noel Coward met Princess Marina, Duchess of Kent and her daughter Princess Alexandra, he noted: "They are *not* pleased over Princess Margaret's engagement. There was a distinct *froideur* when I mentioned it."

Across the Channel in Paris the Duchess of Windsor, the ultimate royal outcast, wryly remarked that "at least I'm keeping up with the Joneses."

Prince Philip gave the bride away, with lip readers noting a typical princely quip as the procession began to move towards the high altar. "Am I holding on to you or you holding on to me?" joked Philip. "I'm holding on to you" was the whispered reply.

Margaret was every inch the fairy princess in a stunningly simple Norman Hartnell gown, made from white silk organza. The all-diamond Poltimore Tiara, newly acquired at auction for a rumoured £5,000, was surmounted by an elaborate hair piece to create the illusion of height for the normally petite bride.

Behind her, eight bridesmaids led by the nine year old Princess Anne wore matching Hartnell gowns, based on the design of one of Margaret's early ballgowns which her late

Margaret was every inch the fairy princess in a stunningly simple Norman Hartnell gown, made from white silk organza.

Looking every inch the fairy tale princess, Margaret and her new husband Antony Armstrong-Jones leave Westminster Abbey at the conclusion of their wedding ceremony. May 6, 1960. Although they remained passionately in love for several years, by the end of the decade they were struggling to keep the marriage alive and they finally separated in 1976.

Queen Elizabeth II addresses a vast gathering of more than a quarter of a million at the Ramlila Grounds, a huge public meeting place outside the walls of Old Delhi, India. It was by far the largest audience ever directly addressed by the Sovereign. January 1961. By now the Queen was far more confident in her role and was able fulfil her personal desire to have more children.

(Opposite) Prince Andrew was born in February 1960 and Elizabeth was able to spend more time with him than she had with the young Charles and Anne.

father, King George VI, had admired.

This was the first royal wedding to be televised live. An estimated 20 million viewers watched in the UK and the world-wide audience was over 300 million. Televising the event meant, in the princess's words: "that those of my friends who couldn't come could still see it. I loved the idea."

There was another royal wedding in June 1961 when the Queen's cousin, Edward, Duke of Kent, married Yorkshire-born Katherine Worsley at York Minster. It was the first royal wedding to take place in the city for 600 years and 2,000 guests filled the Minster.

Among the VIPs was Queen Victoria Eugénie of Spain, grandmother of the present king and a granddaughter of Britain's Queen Victoria.

The Duke continues to serve the royal family, though his Duchess has in recent years dropped her HRH style and as plain Katherine Kent has taught music in a school at Hull. In 2004 Katherine launched, a charity aimed at finding, funding and nurturing musically gifted children. Prior to that she was perhaps best known for presenting the

women's single trophy at Wimbledon and for changing to the Roman Catholic faith in 1994.

At the end of 1961 the Queen visited Ghana on one of her most dangerous visits to date. A bomb blast five days before her arrival had made the visit doubtful, as it was feared the country might be on the brink of revolution.

Elizabeth was however determined to visit. Her PM, Harold Macmillan feared that cancellation would push Ghana out of the Commonwealth and into the arms of the Soviet Union.

The Queen agreed: "If I were to cancel now," she said, "Nkrumah might invite Kruschev, and they wouldn't like that, would they?"

After an audience, during which Elizabeth made it clear how indignant she was that the trip might be cancelled, Macmillan told his Private Secretary how impressed he was with her, "What a girl she is," he said.

As she approached the tenth anniversary of her accession she was finding personal fulfilment in motherhood but also professional satisfaction in her mastery of her role.

Elizabeth had loved horses from being little and had been given her first pony when she was just five. Here she celebrates her tenth birthday with a ride on her new white pony in Windsor Great Park, accompanied by her riding master. April 21, 1936.

Horse & Hounds

At the age of twelve Princess Elizabeth confided that she would one day: "like to be a lady living in the country with lots of horses and dogs."

Horse racing is one of the Queen's chief passions and her expertise in racing and horse breeding is considerable. She has a detailed knowledge of pedigrees and bloodlines and she is an expert judge of any horse.

In over half a century of flat-racing she has won four out of the five English Classics – the only one to elude her is the Derby and it remains an unfulfilled ambition to win this legendary race.

This abiding passion for horses began at an early age. Her grandfather, King George V used to take her around the stud at Sandringham, and in 1931 when she was just five years old, he bought her a Shetland pony called Peggy.

In 1946, at the age of twenty, she shared the ownership of a steeplechaser called Monaveen with her mother Queen Elizabeth. The following year she was given a filly called Astrakhan as a wedding present from the Aga Khan.

Following the death of her father in 1952 the Queen inherited the Royal Studs and the next few years were to be a particularly glorious period for the young royal owner. In 1953 Aureole was the favourite to win that year's Derby. To her disappointment the horse finished second, beaten by Pinza.

The 1970s proved to be the next golden period for the Queen's horses. In 1974 she flew to Chantilly to see Highclere win the prestigious Prix de Diana. Her racing manager, Lord Carnarvon, later recalled the excitement of the French crowd: "they went bananas, shouting 'Vive la reine' when Highclere won." Three years later and the Queen's Silver Jubilee celebrations were capped when Dunfermline, another talented filly, won the Oaks and then the St Leger.

The Queen's Bloodstock and Racing Adviser is John Warren. The royal studs continue to be run from Sandringham and Wolferton in Norfolk and are now managed by Joe Grimwade. The stallions, mares and foals are based here while the weanlings and yearlings are kept at the Polhampton Lodge Stud in Berkshire which was bought by the Queen in 1972.

The Queen's duties often prevent her from seeing her horses in training or racing so she keeps in day to day contact with John Warren and Joe Grimwade, as well as the trainers, and video recordings are made of the races she cannot attend.

Another daily routine is a quick perusal of the Racing Post to see how the competition is faring. If she is out of London this is followed by a morning hacking through the estates of Balmoral, Sandringham or Windsor on one of her favourite mares. These are based at Windsor and are sent on to the other estates in time for the Queen's visits.

Horses may mean the world to the Queen but it is another four-legged animal that is most associated with her in the public's imagination.

The Queen was just seven years old when, in 1933, her parents were given a Pembrokeshire Corgi called Dookie. He was mated with a bitch, Jane, and the royal corgi line was established. The first one owned exclusively by Princess Elizabeth was Susan, who accompanied her owner on her honeymoon in 1947 and whose grave at Sandringham is marked with a small headstone.

The Queen always looks relaxed when she is with her horses & dogs.

(From top left) She enjoys an early morning gallop at Ascot racecourse in June 1961; talking to her corgis while waiting for Prince Philip to take part in the European Carriage Driving Championship at Windsor in May 1973; Arriving at London Airport from Scotland with a posse of corgis in 1962.

(From Left to Right) Standing near the hurdles at Sandown Races with her mother in November 1953; meeting up with an old friend on this 1998 visit to the Roman site of Vindolanda near Hadrian's Wall in Northumberland. This corgi had been bred by the Queen and was now owned by Lady Beaumont who lives in the area; the Queen enjoys a joke as she watches Highland Horses in the Copper Horse Arena during the Royal Windsor Horse Show at Windsor Castle in May 2009.

As with her horses, the Queen meticulously plans the dogs' breeding programme. Something seems to have gone awry in the 1960s when one of them mutinied and mated with Princess Margaret's dachshund to produce Mr Pipkin - the first of the royal 'Dorgis'.

The Queen has owned more than thirty corgis over the years. She is very much a hands-on owner and feeds the dogs herself at 4:30pm each afternoon, mixing cooked meat, gravy and dog biscuits before finally having her own tea. This ritual has remained the same throughout her reign, as has the daily walk around the gardens of the royal estates. In her absence one of the footmen has the unenviable task of taking up to 14 dogs out for a walk at the same time.

As the court moves from residence to residence throughout the year the dogs accompany their mistress, travelling by car, train or aircraft – the only exceptions are royal tours abroad when they are left in the care of Mrs Nancy Fenwick at Windsor, until the Queen's return.

Apart from her corgis and dorgis, the Queen breeds working labradors at her kennels on the Sandringham estate. Whenever she visits she likes to help train the dogs that are used to fetch the birds brought down during shooting parties. The dogs are trained to recognise whistled commands that tell them where the birds have fallen.

The Queen's dogs and horses allow her to relax in a completely different environment to her working life. More importantly they are never obsequious or judgemental and happily none have sold their story to the tabloids – to date!

Prince Edward, fourth child of the Queen and the Duke of Edinburgh, grips the finger of his brother, four-year-old Prince Andrew, as the Queen bends over the baby's crib in the Music Room of Buckingham Palace.

A Second Family

1962 – 1972

Elizabeth was 35 at the start
of her second decade as monarch and was
absorbed with her new, young family.

A Second Family

By the end of the decade the focus was very much on the future, with the launch of Prince Charles and Princess Anne onto the world stage and the Investiture of Charles as Prince of Wales.

Prince Andrew had been born in 1960 and the Queen told a friend: "it's fun having a baby in the house again." Four years later he was joined in the royal nursery by Elizabeth's fourth and final child, Prince Edward.

The decade was a rocky one for the Commonwealth with South Africa declaring independence from Britain and French separatists booing the Queen in Canada. There was more booing during some controversial incoming visits from the monarchs of Greece and Japan.

There were the deaths of two of the Queen's aunts – the Princess Royal and Princess Marina, Duchess of Kent – as well as the passing of Sir Winston Churchill, the defender of Britain during her darkest hour.

By the end of the decade the focus was very much on the future, with the launch of Prince Charles and Princess Anne onto the world stage and the Investiture of Charles as Prince of Wales. There was also the groundbreaking documentary *Royal Family* which for the very first time gave us a behind the scenes glimpse of the royals at work as well as play and an insight into the type of role Charles was being trained for.

On 11 May 1962 Charles began the next phase of his education, following once again in Philip's footsteps by being taught at Gordonstoun, on the Morayshire coast in Scotland. As Prince William was to find a generation later when he enrolled at St Andrew's University, it was a suitable

The Queen celebrates her 39th birthday with a family gathering at Frogmore House in Windsor Great Park. April 21, 1965. With the birth of Prince Edward the year before the family was now complete.

(Opposite) 12 week old Edward makes his first balcony appearance in the arms of his mother after the Trooping the Colour ceremony. June 1964.

(Clockwise from above) The Queen made her second visit to Australia in 1963 and is seen here with Robert Menzies, the Australian Prime Minister at a reception in Parliament House, Canberra.

(Bottom right) The same year Princess Anne is in charge of three-year-old Andrew and one of the family corgis as they prepare to board the royal train en route to the annual summer break on the Balmoral estate.

(Bottom left) Fifteen-year-old Charles wears his Gordonstoun school uniform as he arrives at London's Euston Station before heading to the palace to see his new baby brother Edward for the first time. March 14, 1964.

distance away from the prying eyes of Fleet Street.

For the shy and sensitive Prince of Wales, leaving home was a wrench. He went on record as saying the that he thought of his family as "very special people." "I've never wanted to get away from home," he said, "we happen to be a very close-knit family. I'm happier at home with my family than anywhere else."

He would find the tough, spartan life of Gordonstoun, difficult to cope with. It is said both the Queen and her mother favoured Eton for the sensitive Charles, but, while Elizabeth was ultimately responsible for decisions involving the monarchy, Philip was very much in charge of decisions involving family life.

Charles lived in a block called Windmill Lodge with 59 other pupils. They were woken at 7am, followed by a cold shower and a morning run before lessons. Philip admired the aims of the school's founder, Kurt Hahn, who believed in developing the boys' public service awareness. They were expected to help with local mountain rescue, fire-fighting and coast guard work. The school's motto was 'There is more in you' which sums up the extrovert Philip's attitude to life, probably more than it does Charles's.

The following year, Anne – who would have been ideal for Gordonstoun, but at that time it was only an all-boy school – arrived at Benenden in Kent on 20 September 1963. Until then she had been educated privately at Buckingham Palace. Aged 13, she was apparently sick with fright on the journey to the school and it can't have helped that the entire school of 300 pupils and 14 staff lined up to meet her: more like a royal visit than a first day at boarding school.

There were changes afoot at the palace. Still reeling from the criticism of the late 50s that the monarchy was elitist and out of touch, Prince Philip and courtiers looked at ways of modernising the ancient institution without reducing any of its valuable mystique.

On 25 July 1962 the Queen's Gallery was opened at Buckingham Palace. Long queues formed to see an exhibition called *Treasures of the Royal Collection* which would be followed by *Royal Children* a year later. The gallery was built on the site of the former private chapel,

which had been bombed in 1940. It was the first time the public had been permitted to enter the palace precincts other than to attend investitures or garden party. The fee was two shillings and sixpence (12.5p) and a notice warned them "no other part of the inside of the palace will be seen" after rumours spread that visitors might even catch a glimpse of the royal family walking in the grounds.

The same year Prince Philip risked upsetting the palace old guard by bringing in a business efficiency expert, to help the Duke streamline the cumbersome way the Royal Household was organised. Modern office equipment was installed and an internal phone system revamped to cut back on the traditional method of servants carrying round messages by hand.

Even the normally spendthrift Queen Mother saved a considerable amount by flying to Canada, for her tour in June 1962, on a scheduled commercial airline, becoming the first member of the royal family to do so.

In March 1963 the Queen made her second visit to Australia. The focus of this visit was to mark the fiftieth anniversary of the establishment of the capital Canberra. At a banquet, the Prime Minister Robert Menzies, who had the same fatherly, romantic feeling for Elizabeth, that Churchill had, made a cringing speech, causing the Queen to blush.

"I ask you to remember," he said, "that in this country every man, woman and child who even sees you as a passing glimpse will remember it with joy. In the words of the 17th century poet: 'I did but see her passing by. But yet I love her till I die.'"

Journalists covering the tour were keeping a book on the greatest 'grovel' of the current visit, which also took the Queen to New Zealand.

The days of 'grovelling' were on the decline back home in the UK as satire was on the increase. The irreverent *Private Eye*, first published in 1961, gave many of its covers over to royal images with cheeky captions and speech bubbles.

The popular TV show *That Was The Week That Was* or 'TW3' as it was sometimes called, mocked many of the institutions of the day with comedian Willie Rushton even

A TV audience of 200 million worldwide watched the live ceremony and the procession through the streets of London to the reception at St James's Palace.

imitating the Prime Minister, Harold Macmillan. They were pilloried as "peddlers of filth and smut and destroyers of all that Britain holds dear", but attracted a regular audience of 10 million.

Surprisingly it was Princess Margaret who suggested they include a piece on the royals, which would go down in broadcasting history. She approached Ned Sherrin, the show's producer, at a party, and suggested he should "do a sketch about the absurdly reverential way the press reports us". So the next week the team did a skit about the Queen's barge sinking in the Thames. It was clearly lampooning the fawning style of broadcasters such as Richard Dimbleby who was the voice of many TV royal broadcasts from the Coronation to that year's wedding of Princess Alexandra.

Alexandra, the Queen's popular cousin, known to the family, as 'Pud', married 34 year old city broker, Angus Ogilvy in Westminster Abbey on 24 April 1963. A TV audience of 200 million worldwide watched the live ceremony and the procession through the streets of London to the reception at St James's Palace.

There were negative headlines two months later when 14-year-old Prince Charles was on a school visit to the Hebrides. Arriving at Stornaway, the prince and his group entered the Crown Hotel where, in an effort to avoid the stares of locals through the hotel window, he walked through to the bar and ordered a Cherry Brandy. Unfortunately next to him was a freelance journalist who made the scoop of the year at the expense of Charles, who was disciplined back at Gordonstoun and also lost the services of his favourite protection officer.

The following month there were 94 arrests after angry crowds protested about the visit to the UK of the King and Queen of Greece. Queen Frederika had been a member of the Nazi League of German Girls and had also supported the arrest of left-wing activists in Greece.

During the Greek State Visit, Harold Wilson, the UK Prime Minister, boycotted the State Banquet at Buckingham Palace. Elizabeth was booed as she arrived with the Greek royals for a special performance of *A Midsummer Night's Dream* at a London theatre. There were also shouts of "Sieg Heil" and the Queen was said to be "startled and dismayed."

Later in the decade there were similar protests when Emperor Hirohito of Japan paid a state visit in October 1971, twenty-six years after the end of the war during which his country had subjected British service men and women to barbaric treatment in prisoner of war camps. Seated beside the Emperor in a carriage procession along the Mall, the Queen could hear the comments of the crowd only too clearly. "I'm glad the Emperor couldn't understand English…" she confided later.

For the second time in six years the Queen was embroiled in a Conservative Party succession crisis. In October 1963, Prime Minister Harold Macmillan was struck down by acute prostate trouble and announced that he could not continue in office. After undergoing surgery at London's King Edward VII Hospital for Officers, he tendered his resignation, not at the palace as per usual, but in the library of the hospital, where he had been wheeled down in his bed.

After he told the Queen, "I'm afraid I can't go on," she asked, "Have you any advice to give me?" Macmillan then read out a prepared statement which advocated the Earl of Home as his successor. In order to serve in the Commons, Home would have to lose his peerage and assume the title Sir Alec Douglas Home. The Queen accepted his

The Queen, flanked by princes Philip and Charles, leads a procession of British and European royals through the nave of Westminster Abbey following the wedding of her cousin Princess Alexandra to Angus Ogilvy. April 1963.

The 38-year-old Queen looks happy and relaxed as she poses with her two youngest children at Buckingham Palace. By now she had reigned for twelve years and found it easier to combine her royal duties with the motherhood. June 1964

(Opposite) A reminder of the past as the Queen greets her uncle and aunt the Duke and Duchess of Windsor. The exiled couple were attending a ceremony outside Marlborough House, on The Mall, during which Elizabeth unveiled a plaque to mark the centenary of her grandmother, Queen Mary's birth. It was the first time the Duchess had been present at a formal royal engagement in Britain. June 1967.

advice, but some felt the outgoing PM had behaved unconstitutionally. A member of the royal household said later: "Macmillan was exercising a right he thought he had to advise the Queen on his successor, but technically he hadn't because he had already resigned." Changes in how the Tory party elects its leader internally has meant the same situation will never arise again.

That Christmas of 1963 there were four pregnant royal ladies gathered at Sandringham to celebrate the festivities. The family was now growing so large in numbers that the following year's celebrations had to relocate to Windsor where the royals would spend Christmas every year until 1988 when they returned to Sandringham while the castle was re-wired.

Princess Alexandra gave birth to a leap year baby, James Ogilvy, on 29 February 1964, the Duchess of Kent gave birth to a daughter, Lady Helen Windsor on 28 April and Princess Margaret also had a daughter, Lady Sarah Armstrong-Jones, on 1 May.

The Queen's fourth child, and third son, was born on 10 March 1964, at Buckingham Palace. The Queen who was a month off her 38th birthday had an easy pregnancy and labour and was once again sitting up reading the contents of her daily red boxes within hours.

The new baby was christened Edward Antony Richard Louis in the private chapel of Windsor on 2 May. Edward is a traditional royal name; Antony and Richard are the names of his godfathers the Earl of Snowdon and the Duke of Gloucester, and Louis was in honour of his great uncle Earl Mountbatten of Burma.

In October of 1964 the Queen faced unprecedented security arrangements when on her latest tour of Canada. French-Canadian separatists had detonated bombs in Quebec City prior to the visit as they sought independence from the English-speaking majority. Their leader insisted the demonstrations would be against the federal capital rather than the Queen as a person, so the visit went ahead. Stringent security put many loyalists off lining the streets and for the most part the Queen drove past empty sections of the city.

Across the globe, a continuing Commonwealth problem was Southern Rhodesia, now Zimbabwe. In November 1965 Ian Smith, leader of the Rhodesian Front party, who opposed black majority rule in the British colony, signed a unilateral declaration of independence of Rhodesia from the UK.

As with Canada it was made clear that it was meant with no disrespect to the Queen as a person. In fact Smith went as far as regarding Elizabeth as a separate entity to her government. The Queen however refused to accept the title of Queen of Rhodesia and four year later the African state voted to declare itself a republic.

In January there was a poignant reminder of Britain's past with the death of Sir Winston Churchill at the age of ninety. The Queen approved plans for a state funeral and his body lay in Westminster Hall where more than 300,000 people filed past. At St Paul's Cathedral the Queen, in the words of Churchill's daughter, Mary Soames, "waiving all precedence, awaited the arrival of her greatest subject." The monarch had sent her first Prime Minister six half bottles of non-vintage champagne on his deathbed. At his graveside at Bladon in Oxfordshire, a wreath of white flowers bore the message, in her own handwriting: "From the Nation and the Commonwealth. In grateful remembrance. Elizabeth R."

Two months later there was another personal loss, with the sudden death of Elizabeth's Aunt Mary, the Princess Royal, the only daughter of King George V and Queen Mary. She collapsed and died of a heart attack in the grounds of Harewood House, her home near Leeds. The Queen and other members of the Royal Family travelled to Yorkshire in the royal train for the funeral service.

The same month Elizabeth met her uncle, the Duke of Windsor, for the first time in over a decade, while he was in the London Clinic for an eye operation. More significantly she also met her aunt, the Duchess, face to face for the first time since 1936. The previous June, the Queen greatly cheered the Duke by sending him a telegram congratulating him on his 70th birthday, which undoubtedly helped heal the rift in the family caused by the Abdication.

On 7 June 1967, the Windsors were invited by the Queen to attend the unveiling of a memorial plaque at Marlborough House, just off the Mall, in memory of Queen Mary. The Duke and Queen Mary's only other surviving child, the Duke of Gloucester, were both present. More significantly the Duchess was also part of the royal party. It was a tense occasion. The Duchess did not curtsey but bowed to the Queen and shook hands with the Queen Mother. The Queen kissed her uncle, as did the Queen Mother.

The Duke returned for the next royal occasion, the funeral of Princess Marina in 1968, on his own. The Queen did however urge younger members of the family to visit the Windsors whenever they were in France. In October 1970, Prince Charles called into see them after attending a shoot in the Paris area.

In May of 1965 the Queen visited Germany, twenty years after the end of Churchill's war. During her 11 day, and ten-city tour she rode in an open-topped car alongside the Berlin Wall erected by the East German nation to stop its citizens fleeing to the west.

It was the first royal visit to Germany since her grandfather George V was a guest of his cousin Kaiser Wilhelm II in 1913. Elizabeth is a direct descendant of the Elector Georg of Hanover, who succeeded to the British throne as George I, and she was estimated to have 400 distant relatives living in Germany.

In January there was a poignant reminder of Britain's past with the death of Sir Winston Churchill at the age of ninety.

The Queen and Prince Philip lead the procession out of St Paul's Cathedral following the State Funeral of Sir Winston Churchill. Behind the royal couple are the Queen Mother and Prince Charles, Princess Margaret and her husband Lord Snowdon, the Duke and Duchess of Gloucester and the Princess Royal. January 30, 1965.

The Beatles after receiving their MBE's from the Queen. (L-R) Ringo Starr, John Lennon, Paul McCartney and George Harrison. The honour wasn't popular in all quarters and several previous recipients returned their own medals to the palace in protest. October 1965.

(Opposite) The Queen presents the Jules Rimet Trophy to the England captain Bobby Moore after he had led his team to a 4-2 victory over Germany in the exciting World Cup Final at Wembley. Further along the royal box, the Duke Of Edinburgh and the Duchess of Kent look clearly delighted with the outcome of the match. July 1966.

It was now the middle of the swinging sixties and among the usual establishment figures that annually receive honours from the sovereign was the pop group that had taken the music world by storm – The Beatles. The Queen presented each of the Fab Four with an MBE. When she asked: "How long have you been together as a band?" John Lennon replied with the lyrics of the old music hall song: "We've been together now for forty years, and it doesn't seem a day too much." Lennon also recalled her response: "she had this strange quizzical look on her face, like she wanted to laugh or she was thinking 'off with their heads.'" Their MBEs made an appearance two years later on the cover of their eighth album, *Sergeant Pepper's Lonely Hearts Club Band.*

On 22 December 1965 an advisory committee made up of the Prime Minister, Harold Wilson, the Archbishop of Canterbury, Earl Mountbatten, the Dean of Windsor and the Chairman of the Committee of Vice-Chancellors met for dinner with the Queen and the Duke to discuss the future of the Prince of Wales, although the 17 year old Charles was not invited to join them.

It was decided that he should go to Trinity College, Cambridge, but before then he was already committed to a lengthy stay in Australia at a school called Timbertop in the bush country 200 miles (320 km) north of Melbourne. This was an outpost of Geelong Grammar School and the idea was for Charles to broaden his education and at the same time to learn more about Australia. He lived in a hut as a prefect-supervisor of 14 younger boys, and as part of the curriculum would take them on outward-bound ventures including long hikes and camping in the bush.

While he was there he was visited by the Queen Mother, who was on her first visit to Australia and New Zealand since 1927. The royal matriarch indulged in her love of fishing, especially in New Zealand. A two day expedition on North Island only produced one small fish and she joked: "it would have been better to have got one out of the deep freeze."

Meanwhile the Queen was touring much nearer to home, on a two-day visit to Belfast in July 1966. While she was driving through the city with the Duke she escaped injury when a concrete block was thrown from an office building and hit the bonnet of her limousine. Unfazed by the incident, she later inspected damage to the vehicle and said nonchalantly, "it's a strong car." Two people were later arrested and the Prime Minister faced questions in parliament about her security.

On a more positive note that same month the Queen was at Wembley to watch England's 4-2 victory against Germany in the World Cup. Bobby Moore, the victorious captain was seen wiping the mud off his hands on the sides of the decorated royal box before shaking hands with the Queen and accepting the Jules Rimet Trophy from her.

On 21 October 1966 a coal tip collapsed in the mining village of Aberfan in South Wales, killing 144 people, including 116 children. The Duke of Edinburgh and Lord Snowdon visited almost immediately but the Queen held back and would later regard this as a big mistake.

When she did go, six days after the accident, she spent two and a half hours with families and rescuers. She told

"She was very upset. She was the most charming person
I have ever met in my entire life.
Really down to earth."

the bereaved: "As a mother, I'm trying to understand what your feelings must be," adding "I'm sorry I can't give you anything at present except sympathy." After placing a wreath at the cemetery where 81 of the children were buried, she took tea with Councillor Jim Williams who had lost seven relatives. His wife later said: "She was very upset. She was the most charming person I have ever met in my entire life. Really down to earth."

By now some of the palace old guard were retiring. Sir Richard Colville, her formidable Press Secretary was one of them. Known as the 'Abominable No-man' for his unhelpful attitude to the press and, ironically, 'Smiler' by those who worked with him, Colville was replaced by William Heseltine, a more down to earth Australian with a better understanding of the modern media.

Under Heseltine and his team, the palace made better use of the opportunities TV afforded. In July 1967 for instance, when the Queen knighted Francis Chichester, the round the world yachtsman, she did so at Greenwich in public, using the sword with which Elizabeth I knighted Francis Drake. Later in the year her Christmas broadcast was shown in colour for the first time.

It was however a more major project that Heseltine had in mind – a behind-the-scenes TV documentary on how the monarchy functions. Before approaching the Queen he won over Earl Mountbatten and his film producer son-in-law Lord Brabourne as well as Prince Philip.

Heseltine was, in his own words: "concerned that people had no notion of the Queen and Prince Philip's personalities...There was also a public perception that their eldest two children were slightly dull, perhaps even slightly retarded."

Prince Philip also had his concerns that the monarchy

was becoming rather stale, "we're getting on for middle-age," he commented in 1968, "and I would have thought we were entering the least interesting period."

The Investiture of the Prince of Wales at Caernarvon on 1 July 1969 was seen as a useful peg to hang the documentary on, and it was decided to show the world the work the monarchy does and the role that he would one day succeed to.

A seven-man film crew was drawn up under the leadership of Richard Cawston, and filming began with the Trooping the Colour in June 1968.

The Queen was initially reluctant to take part. "It's no good, I'm not a film star," she told Heseltine, and she was concerned that people might think the resulting film might be too boring to watch.

In the end she proved a natural and the public, used only to seeing the Queen making formal speeches, lapped up sequences where she helped make a salad dressing, went into a shop to buy Prince Edward an ice cream and helped decorate the family Christmas tree.

Before the film was released the royal family were given a special screening. It had been agreed all along that they had the right of veto and Dick Cawston was worried that they might axe scene after scene. In the event it was passed in its entirety, though Prince Philip was concerned about the scene where a string on Prince Charles's cello snaps and stings Edward in the face making him cry. In the end the Duke was persuaded it added to the naturalness of the whole programme.

Forty years ago, 23 million people tuned into BBC 1 to watch a landmark documentary that covered a year in the life of the Queen and her family.

By the time it was screened on ITV a week later, a total

The Queen appears visibly moved as she views the destruction to the village of Aberfan after a catastrophic collapse of a colliery spoil tip which killed 116 children and 28 adults. Behind her Prince Philip looks at a damaged building to their left.

The Queen and her eldest son the Prince of Wales pose for an informal shot on the terrace at Windsor Castle to mark his forthcoming Investiture.

(Opposite) The ceremony was held at Caernarvon Castle in north Wales and was the first major royal event to be televised in colour. July 1, 1969.

of 30.69 million viewers had been glued to their sets for the 110 minute film and were rewarded with a tantalising glimpse of the first family off duty as well as on the public stage.

Even today *Royal Family* holds the record for the third largest TV audience ever recorded in Britain, beaten only by the audiences for the 1966 World Cup and the funeral of Diana, Princess of Wales.

Colour TV was also taken into account at Charles's Investiture on 1 July 1969 since the ceremony was to be broadcast to an international audience of 500 million people. A perspex canopy embossed with the Prince of Wales feathers and supported by pikestaffs was designed by the prince's uncle Lord Snowdon, "just like Henry V would have done it if he'd had perspex." Guests, including American President Nixon's daughter Tricia, sat on typically stark 1960s style red wood chairs, which could be purchased afterwards for £12 each to defray the cost of the event. They were designed to add contrast with the freshly laid green turf.

Opposition to the event from Welsh Nationalists was extreme, and on the morning of the Investiture, two men were killed while trying to plant a bomb. Fortunately the procession of open-topped royal carriages arrived safely, though an egg thrown by someone in the crowd glanced off the side of the Queen's carriage.

Prince Charles was deeply affected by the occasion and later wrote: "by far the most moving and meaningful moment came when I put my hands between Mummy's and swore to be her liege man of life and limb and to live and die against all manner of folks – such magnificent and medieval appropriate words." His account of the day is balanced with humour as he notes that when the Queen formally presented him to the people of Wales from Queen Eleanor's Gate, they "looked straight down on the public conveniences and a lot of police and TV vans."

Finance was a growing problem for the royal family and at the end of 1969 Prince Philip memorably said, in an interview with America's NBC network, that the monarchy was in danger of going 'into the red.' The Queen's

allowance of £475,000 was, as he pointed out, set up at the beginning of the reign and, as it looked like hers might be a long one, it needed to be revised.

In December 1971 parliament voted the first increase in the Civil List since Elizabeth's accession and the Queen's allowance was more or less doubled to £980,000. This followed a study of royal finances by an all-party Commons committee set up in 1970 by Harold Wilson.

In 1970 another palace initiative proved popular. While she was on a tour of New Zealand, the Queen started a new royal ritual – 'the walkabout' – where instead of merely walking or driving past crowds she stopped to chat to them and to accept flowers and other gifts. Back home she carried out her first one in the UK on a visit to Coventry in June and of course they have continued ever since.

Prince Charles accompanied his parent on the 1970 New Zealand tour. He and Anne were still in the process of being launched on the world's stage, undertaking tours firstly with their parents, then together as brother and sister and finally alone. Their joint visit to the United States in July 1970 as guests of President Richard Nixon was far from successful with Anne being critiqued as "gauche and impatient." It didn't help that she called the bald eagle "rather a bad choice" as the American national symbol.

On their own they seemed to do better. Charles had a successful tour of Japan in April 1970 – his first solo visit

The Queen wears a striking white hat decorated with white ribbons as she opens the £7 million Walsgrave Hospital on the outskirts of Coventry. June 1970.

(Opposite) The previous November, Prince Philip took part in a Meet the Press interview on America's NBC network. He declared the monarchy would soon be 'going into the red' as the Civil List payment which financed the royal family had been set in 1952 and was proving inadequate.

The Queen made a rare visit to Chequers, the British Prime Minister's official country residence in Buckinghamshire, to meet the US President Richard Nixon and his wife Pat. Edward Heath, the Prime Minister stands on the Queen's right. The Nixon's were on a flying visit to England as part of the President's European tour. October 1970.

(Opposite) The Queen with Princess Anne and Prince Charles as they pass through the crowds at the Royal Easter Show in Sydney during the Royal Tour of Australasia. The Queen's eldest two children accompanied her on several tours during this period as part of their training in royal duties.

*Princess Anne was developing into a
skilled equestrian. In April 1971 she came fifth in
the Badminton Horse Trials.*

aboard, when he attended the international trade fare
Expo 70 in Tokyo.

Later in the year he began a flying course at RAF
Benson, Oxfordshire and in August 1971 was presented
with his RAF wings by Prince Philip at RAF Cranwell. His
instructors said he had a natural aptitude for flying and it
was remarked he would make "an excellent fighter pilot at
supersonic speeds."

Princess Anne was developing into a skilled equestrian.
In April 1971 she came fifth in the Badminton Horse
Trials. Then despite having had an operation to remove an
ovarian cyst in July, she was well enough to take part in
the European three-day eventing championships at Burgle

in September. The Queen broke off her summer holidays
at Balmoral to watch her daughter win the individual
champion's title and afterwards presented her with the
winner's trophy and a kiss.

In November she was named Sportswoman of the Year
by the national press and in December was voted BBC
Sports Personality of the Year.

For the Queen the second decade of her reign ended
with her two eldest children both establishing a firm base
to begin their adult lives, and throughout the next ten years
they would bring their own particular strengths to the
family team.

Marilyn Monroe, shaking hands with
Queen Elizabeth II on the occasion of
the 1956 Royal Film Performance of
The Battle of the River Plate, at the
Empire Theatre, Leicester Square.
October 1956.

Queen of the Entertainment World

During these years she has seen thousands of stars from Marilyn Monroe to Lady Gaga.

Several years ago the Queen was sitting for a portrait at Buckingham Palace. The anxious young artist apologised for making her keep the same rigid pose for over an hour. "Don't worry," said the monarch reassuringly, "I'm used to it. I've had to sit through the Royal Variety Performance nearly every year."

The Queen's parents, King George VI and Queen Elizabeth, were both lovers of variety acts and radio shows such as *ITMA* and they were more than happy to take over as royal patrons. In 1945 they were joined by the princesses Elizabeth and Margaret in what would be the first of Elizabeth's 36 appearances to date.

Elizabeth regularly visited the theatre when she was courting Prince Philip. Back in 1947 it was rumoured that the young lovers had been to see *Oklahoma* time and again and that *People Will Say We're in Love* was their song. Half a century later, to mark the royal couple's Golden Wedding, legendary Broadway star Barbara Cook was flown over especially to duet the number with Michael Ball. Afterwards, meeting the line-up of stars, the Duke shook hands with Ball and said: "You were the chap that sang that special song weren't you? Well I've never heard it in my life."

These days she still occasionally slips into London theatres just before the curtain goes up and two of her recent favourites were *Billy Elliot - the Musical* and *War Horse*.

Like her mother, the Queen has always had a soft spot for British comedians and variety acts from the golden age of television; stars who manage to be both cheeky as well as deferential when it comes to dealing with the royals. Tommy Cooper was a particular

favourite and during one backstage meet and greet he asked the Queen: "Will you be going to the Cup Final next year?" The Queen thought for a moment before replying, "no I don't think I am", to which Cooper quipped back, "well can I have your tickets?" Danny La Rue always fascinated the royals and after the 1969 show the Queen told him: "my goodness your costume changes were fantastic, I only wish I could dress as quickly as you."

When the Kwa Zulu African song and dance company were due to appear in the 1975 show, presenter Bernard Delfont was unsure whether the women in the company should appear topless as they did in their West End show. He took the precautionary measure of writing to the Palace to check out the royal reaction. "Don't worry," came the reply, "the Queen has seen topless ladies before."

The Royal Film Performance is always held in aid of the Cinema and Television Benevolent Fund and the Queen, as the charity's patron, has seen the proceeds from the event escalate from around £30,000 in its earlier years to a staggering half a million pounds on two recent occasions.

Besides raising money, this red carpet event is an opportunity for A-list stars and executives to have a rare brush with the greatest, and most enduring star of them all, the Queen herself.

Harry Myers, who for half a century was the fundraiser's official photographer, recalls the impact of the royal party: "At each and every premier I noticed just how much in awe of the royal patron the stars were, in particular the Queen. No matter how famous they were, they held her in total reverence."

What is striking looking back at photographs from the early years is the formality of the occasion, with the royal ladies and many of the guests wearing furs, elaborate gowns

(L-R) The Queen shakes hands with Tom Jones after the Royal Variety Performance at the London Palladium, England. Also in the line up are entertainer Kenny Lynch, second right, singer Shirley Bassey, third right, and actor and songwriter Anthony Newley. November 24, 1987.

A cheeky grin from Barry Humphries aka Dame Edna Everage, at the Festival Theatre in Edinburgh for the start of the 75th Royal Variety performance in 2003.

The Queen enjoying a joke with Bob Hope in the foyer of London's Palladium Theatre after the 1962 Royal Variety show.

(L-R) The Queen meeting the Spice Girls in 1997. Her Majesty is shaking hands with Geri Halliwell (Ginger Spice) at London's Victoria Palace Theatre.

The flamboyant singer Lady Gaga meets the Queen after the 2009 Royal Variety Performance in Blackpool.

Talking to American singer Lovelace Watkins at the 1971 performance watched by Carry On star Sid James (left) and comedian Tommy Cooper, (right).

and every conceivable type of jewellery and with many of the men in white tie. At the 1964 performance of *Born Free*, it was noted that the Queen wore the ribbon of the Order of the Garter with the diamond encrusted Family Orders as well as a diamond and emerald tiara.

Another striking factor is the calibre of A- list stars that have attended the event over the years. At the 1956 premier of *The Battle of the River Plate*, the Queen was introduced to three of the most famous screen beauties, Joan Crawford, Brigitte Bardot and Marilyn Monroe. Sadly the calibre of the films rarely matched the audiences and after watching Robert Morley's hammy impersonation of her 'mad' ancestor King George III in the 1954 film *Beau Brummell*, the Queen complained to her Prime Minster Winston Churchill who intervened on her behalf to make sure she was never embarrassed in the same way again.

The new millennium has witnessed some of the most spectacular premieres. In 2002 the venue for the royal film was changed to the Royal Albert Hall, which was temporarily transformed into an ice palace for the launch of the James Bond film Die Another Day. A host of A-list stars turned out for the event and while the crowd outside became hysterically star-struck the Queen seemed endearingly vague when faced with the stellar cast. Shaking hands with Pierce Brosnan, who was playing 007 at the time, the Queen seemed taken aback, "but I've just met two James Bonds downstairs." A few moments earlier, Madonna received an equally blank stare and the comment, "oh you sang the song, did you?"

While the actors may come and go and, thankfully, so have some of the films, one attendee remains constant - the Queen, whose main motive is to support the benevolent fund of which she has been patron since 1952. She gamely plays her part to perfection and never fails to recreate an Oscar winning performance year after year.

The official group photo at the wedding of the Prince of Wales to Lady Diana Spencer. Amongst the guests pictured are the Queen, the Queen Mother, Duke of Edinburgh, Princess Anne, Princess Margaret and Earl Spencer. July 29, 1981.

A
Time of Change

1972 – 1982

———◆———

*The Queen's third decade
as monarch was dominated
by family events.*

A Time of Change

The Queen's third decade as monarch was dominated by family events. In 1972 she and Prince Philip celebrated their silver wedding anniversary with a service of thanksgiving at Westminster Abbey.

The following year Princess Anne became the first of Elizabeth's children to marry and, four years later the first to make her a grandmother.

On a sadder note the decade saw the deaths of the Queen's uncles, the Dukes of Windsor and Gloucester, as well as the separation and divorce of Princess Margaret.

The unexpected highlight for the Queen and the country was the celebration of her Silver Jubilee in 1977. Given the poor economic climate at the time it was expected to be a damp squib, but during the year public interest grew and grew and by the summer Britain was basking in Jubilee fever as well as glorious sunshine.

Her third decade ended with one of the most spectacular royal events of the 20th Century, the wedding of the Prince of Wales to Lady Diana Spencer, which gave Britain not only a new princess but a global superstar who would reinvigorate the monarchy.

On 21 January 1972, two weeks before Elizabeth's twentieth anniversary as monarch, her sixth Prime Minister, Edward Heath, signed the Treaty of Accession, making Britain a part of what was then called the European Economic Community (EEC).

With the focus very much on Europe it was decided that the Queen should make a State Visit to France in May 1972 to improve relations between the two countries.

Her itinerary included a courtesy call on her uncle and aunt, the Duke and Duchess of Windsor, who lived in a mansion on Paris's Bois de Boulogne. The Duke was suffering from inoperable cancer of the throat and Elizabeth knew this would not only be her final meeting with the man she had adored as a child, but also the curtain on the Abdication crisis and the ensuing family rift that had lasted for more than three decades.

The Duke's health began to fail and the British Ambassador, Sir Christopher Soames, a son-in-law of Winston Churchill's, made a series of anxious calls to Edward's doctor, Jean Thin. "The Ambassador came to the point," Thin later recalled, "and told me bluntly that it was all right for the Duke to die before or after the visit, but that it would be politically disastrous if he were to expire in the course of it."

In the event the Duke did survive and on the fourth day of the State Visit, the Queen, Prince Philip and Prince Charles called in to see him. By now the former king was bedridden and on an intravenous drip. He insisted, however, that for this special moment he should be dressed and placed in a chair in his sitting room. Elizabeth came in to see him alone and, with supreme effort, the dying man stood and made a bow to her.

According to Dr Thin "they chatted affectionately for about a quarter of an hour," before Elizabeth returned downstairs for tea with the Duchess before posing on the steps of the mansion for a press photograph to record the historic occasion.

Nine days later, on 28 May, the Duke died. Four years earlier, after the funeral of his sister in law, Princess

Her third decade ended with one of the most spectacular Royal events of the 20th Century, the wedding of the Prince of Wales to Lady Diana Spencer.

The Queen and Duke of Edinburgh reading goodwill messages as they celebrate their Silver Wedding Anniversary in the Belgian suite in Buckingham Palace. November 20, 1972.

(Above) The Queen waving to the crowd as she arrives at Longchamp Race Course near Paris, during her State Visit. May 18, 1972.

(Left) While in Paris she took the opportunity to pay a farewell visit to the dying Duke of Windsor and afterwards posed for photos outside the Windsors mansion on the Bois de Bologne with the Duchess.

(Opposite) A month later and the Queen pauses to talk to her aunt, the Duchess of Windsor, following the Duke's funeral at St George's Chapel, Windsor. Prince Philip and the Queen Mother also attended.

Marina, Edward had asked the Queen if he and Wallis could be buried in the royal family's private burial ground at Frogmore, Windsor. Elizabeth agreed to the request and it was here that his body was interred after a lying in state followed by a funeral service in St George's Chapel.

A frail Wallis stayed at Buckingham Palace where a photograph was taken of her haunted face looking out across The Mall as she watched the Queen set off for the Trooping the Colour ceremony. As she prepared for the funeral at Windsor she told Earl Mountbatten: "He was my entire life. I can't begin to think what I am going to do without him. He gave up so much for me and now he has gone."

Two months later the Queen was once again in family mourning, after the tragic death of her cousin, Prince William of Gloucester, in a flying accident on 28 August. The 30-year-old prince was ninth in line to the throne.

A keen amateur pilot since his undergraduate days at Cambridge, William was at the controls of a Piper Cherokee Arrow 200. He and co-pilot Vyrell Mitchell were taking part in an air race near Wolverhampton.

A month earlier he had been best man at the wedding of his younger brother, Prince Richard, to Birgitte van Deurs. Richard, who was expecting to concentrate on a career in architecture, now found himself sole heir to his ailing father, the Duke of Gloucester. He succeeded to the title on 10 June 1974 following the Duke's death at the age of 74. Four months later his son and heir, Alexander, Earl of Ulster, was born in London on 24 October.

On a brighter note, the Queen and Prince Philip celebrated their Silver Wedding on 20 November 1972. The couple drove to Westminster Abbey for a thanksgiving service attended by members of the royal family. Afterwards they shared a carriage with their eldest two children for the procession to the Guildhall in the City of London.

During her address the Queen poked fun at her oft-parodied style of beginning similar speeches. "I think that everybody really will agree that on this, of all days, I should begin my speech with the words, 'My Husband and I.'"

She added: "If I am asked today what I think about family life after twenty five years of marriage, I can answer

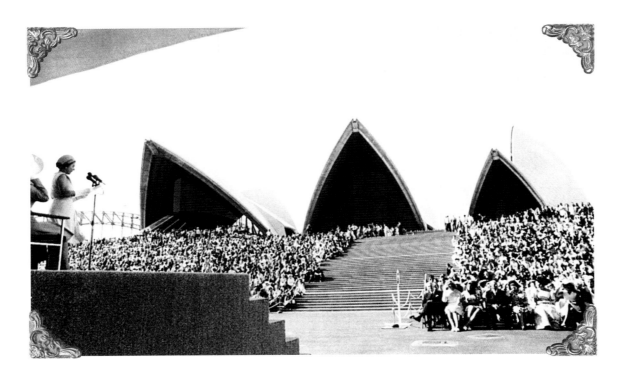

with simplicity and conviction, I am for it."

After the official lunch, hosted by the Lord Mayor of London, the Queen and Duke carried out a walkabout among the crowds outside – their first major one in the capital.

Britain's entry into the EEC took effect from 1 January 1973, so one of the aims of the Queen's Christmas broadcast a week earlier was to reassure the Commonwealth of her continued support. "The new links with Europe will not replace those with the Commonwealth," she said, "They cannot alter our historical ties and personal attachments with kinsmen and friends overseas. Old friends will not be lost. Britain will take her Commonwealth links into Europe with her."

It was inevitable that the ties would weaken, but Elizabeth was concerned when newspaper editorials in Canada theorised as to whether the time had come to think of having a head of state of Canadian extraction.

There was a also clear weakening of her position in Australia in 1973 when, during her six-day tour, the

Queen signed the Royal Styles and Titles Bill. This stated that when she was in Australia, she would be referred to as 'Queen of Australia' and not, as she had hitherto been known, 'Queen of the United Kingdom of Great Britain and of Her Other Realms and Territories.'

The other purpose of the Australian visit was to officially open the Sydney Opera House, built at a cost of AUS $102 million, on 20 October. A massive firework display followed the opening accompanied by Beethoven's ninth symphony and the spectacular event was shown live on television throughout the world.

In November 1973 Princess Anne became the first of the Queen's children to marry. Rumours of a royal romance with fellow equestrian, Mark Phillips, had been circulating in the press since the beginning of the year. In February Anne herself told journalists: "We are not engaged and there is no prospect of an engagement."

The princess must have had a change of heart since, on 29 May, it was announced from Buckingham Palace: "It is with the greatest pleasure that The Queen and the Duke

The Queen looks every inch the proud mother as she attends Princess Anne's wedding to Captain Mark Phillips in Westminster Abbey accompanied by the Queen Mother and princes Charles and Andrew. November 14, 1973.

(Opposite) Declaring open the Sydney Opera House complex in front of an audience of 15,000 invited guests. October 20, 1973.

Three generations at the christening of Princess Anne's 37 day old son Peter Phillips, at Buckingham Palace. Peter is the eldest of the Queen's eight grandchildren and was born during her Silver Jubilee year. December 22, 1977.

(Opposite) A curtsey for her mother and sovereign from Princess Anne during her wedding at Westminster Abbey. Mark Phillip's father, mother and sister are on the left of the front row as they watch him bow to the Queen. November 1973.

of Edinburgh announce the betrothal of their beloved daughter The Princess Anne to Lieutenant Mark Phillips." 25 year old Mark, who was two years older than the princess, had been educated at Marlborough College and trained at Sandhurst before joining the Guards in 1969.

The couple shared a love of horses, and in particular of equestrianism, prompting the Queen to joke: "I shouldn't wonder if their children are four-legged," and the Queen Mother to quip: "They could almost have been computer-dated."

The wedding took place on 14 November, Prince Charles's 25th birthday, at Westminster Abbey, watched by a congregation of 1,800 and a TV audience estimated at 500 million.

Anne wore an embroidered Tudor-style wedding dress with a high collar and mediaeval sleeves, designed by Susan Small. Having been chief bridesmaid several times, Anne had painful memories of what she referred to as "yards of uncontrollable children." As a consequence she opted for just two attendants, her cousin, Lady Sarah-Armstrong

Jones, daughter of Princess Margaret, and her brother Prince Edward, both aged nine.

The wedding day had been declared a national holiday and crowds lined the streets to watch the newly married couple on their way back to Buckingham Palace. Later on the couple departed by carriage for their overnight stay at White House Lodge in Richmond Park, prior to joining the Royal Yacht *Britannia* in Barbados for an 18 day cruise.

Four months after their marriage, Anne and Mark were involved in a terrifying kidnap attempt as they were returning to Buckingham Palace from an evening engagement on 20 March 1974. As the royal limousine was heading down the Mall, a Ford Escort swerved in front of it, forcing it to screech to a halt. A man called Ian Ball fired shots at the car and tried to force Anne to come with him. The princess refused and Mark hung on to her arm, ripping her dress in the process. Eventually Ball was overpowered by a police officer after shooting four people including Anne's protection officer James Beaton, who was later awarded the George Cross by the Queen.

In 1976 the Queen bought the couple Gatcombe Park, set in 733 acres of the Gloucestershire countryside, as a belated wedding present.

On 15 November 1977, the day after her fourth wedding anniversary, Anne gave her mother her first grandson, Peter Mark Andrew Phillips. That morning the Queen was to hold an Investiture at Buckingham Palace. She apologised for being ten minutes late, telling the recipients and their families: "I have just had a message from the hospital. My daughter has given birth to a son, and I am now a grandmother."

Three and a half year's later, Anne gave birth to Zara Anne Elizabeth, the Queen's first granddaughter, on 15 May 1981.

The issue of the Queen's involvement with the Commonwealth came to a head again in 1975 when her representative in Australia, Sir John Kerr, plunged that country into a constitutional crisis.

In November of that year the Opposition leader, Sir Malcolm Fraser, used his majority in the Australian Senate to block the Labour Government's Budget Bills. Sir John, the then Governor-General, dismissed the Prime Minister, Gough Whitlam, and appointed Fraser as acting premier in his place. The whole issue of the Queen's involvement in Australian politics was highlighted and examined.

Buckingham Palace revealed that the Queen had been kept informed of what was happening in preceding weeks, but was at pains to point out, that Kerr had not told her about Whitlam's dismissal until after it happened. Kerr said this was to protect the monarch, and he was supposed to have told her later, "Governor-Generals are expendable. The Queen is not."

In March 1976 the Queen was greatly saddened by her sister's decision to end her sixteen-year marriage. Princess Margaret and Lord Snowdon had been the darlings of the London society during the 'Swinging Sixties' but by the end of the decade their relationship was becoming increasingly volatile and both of them had experienced affairs.

In 1973 the forty three year old princess began seeing 25-year-old Roddy Llewellyn, who had been introduced to her by her lady-in-waiting, Anne Tennant, and her husband Colin.

Early in 1976 the affair became public when a photograph of Margaret and Roddy in bathing costumes, taken near her holiday home on the Caribbean island of Mustique appeared in the *News of the World*. The newspaper had cropped out the princess's friends to make the captured moment look far more intimate than it actually was.

The photograph was the catalyst that ended the marriage. A few days later a statement was issued from Margaret's office informing the world that the Snowdons "have mutually agreed to live apart. The Princess will carry out her public duties and functions unaccompanied by Lord Snowdon. There are no plans for divorce proceedings."

Elizabeth's Press Secretary told the media: "The Queen is naturally very sad at what happened." Her main concern was for the welfare of the Snowdon's two children David, Viscount Linley, then aged fourteen and his twelve year old sister Lady Sarah Armstrong Jones. They would often stay with either her or the Queen Mother and would continue to be close to their aunt even up to the present day. They are invited to spend Christmas at Sandringham with their royal relations every year.

Margaret's relationship with Roddy ended in 1981 when the latter left her to marry Tania Soskin. Three years before, contrary to the earlier public statement, the Snowdon marriage had ended in divorce on the grounds that the couple had lived apart for two years. Margaret was granted custody of their two children.

On 21 April 1976 the Queen celebrated her 50th birthday at Windsor, with a party for fifty close friends and family, followed by a ball for 500 guests. On the day itself she hosted a tea party for the 180 members of the Victoria Cross and George Cross Association in the State Apartments.

That summer Elizabeth undertook one of her most historic tours when she visited the United States to celebrate its bicentenary of the signing of the Declaration of Independence from Britain.

The Queen smiles for the camera as she celebrates her 50th birthday with Prince Philip and their twelve-year-old son Prince Edward in the grounds of Windsor Castle. April 21, 1976.

The Queen paid a State Visit to the USA in July 1976 to mark the bicentennial of independence from Britain.

(Clockwise from the top) The royal couple acknowledge the crowd from the balcony of the White House in Washington where they were greeted by President Gerald Ford and his wife Betty.

(Bottom Right) Sightseeing at the Lincoln Memorial.

(Bottom Left) An apprehensive Mr Ford dances with the Queen in the State Dining Room following dinner at the White House.

(Opposite) The Queen smiles at Girl Scouts, dressed in colonial garb, as they present a book on American woman to the royal visitors in Philadelphia, July 6, 1976.

The heat in Philadelphia and Washington was intense with temperatures staying at 100 degrees Fahrenheit even during the night. President Gerald Ford hosted a White House dinner for the royal visitors and Elizabeth was filmed dancing a foxtrot in the ballroom to the wildly inappropriate tune of *The Lady is a Tramp*.

Elizabeth gave a return dinner at the British Embassy in Washington attended by a host of famous faces, and best remembered today for being the occasion when Elizabeth Taylor fell in love with her escort for the evening, Senator John Warner, who became the actress's sixth husband the following December.

Susan Crosland, wife of the UK Foreign Secretary Anthony Crosland, accompanied the royal party and later recalled: "The Queen never faltered in the day's walkabout under a remorseless sun, crowds stretching their arms out to her."

Elizabeth gave Mrs Crosland her tips on how to stand for hours without tiring. "One plants one's feet like this," said the Queen, hitching her evening gown above her ankles. "Always keep them parallel. Make sure your weight is evenly distributed. That's all there is to it."

After visiting America, the Queen headed to Canada to officially open the Montreal Olympics – in both French and English - on 17 July 1976. Despite fears of protests from French Separatists, the ceremony went without a hitch; largely due to what were called 'tighter than tight' security measures to avoid a repeat of the tragedy of the 1972 Munich games when eleven Israeli athletes were killed by Palestinian gunmen.

The Queen stayed on to watch Princess Anne and Captain Phillips compete as part of the British Equestrian team. The royal couple insisted on being treated the same as any other competitors, flying economy class and queuing for the buffet.

Mark was relegated to the reserve list and did not compete. Anne took part and while riding in the cross-country section she fell and was knocked unconscious in front of the Queen. She recovered to take part in the following day's show jumping, and finished a creditable fourth.

1977 was dominated by the Queen's Silver Jubilee celebrations. On the actual anniversary of her accession, 6 February, she spent the day quietly at Windsor where she attended a church service with her mother and sister at the tiny All Saints Church next to Royal Lodge.

Four days later she set off on the first of two overseas Jubilee tours. This one took her and Prince Philip to Fiji, Samoa, Papua New Guinea, New Zealand and Australia.

During the year she would travel over 56,000 miles both in the UK and overseas, ending her travels in October with a tour of Canada and the West Indies, and a return flight on Concorde.

In Britain the celebrations included a gala concert at Covent Garden, the lighting of a chain of beacons from Windsor Castle to the remotest islands of Scotland, a naval review off Spithead, and her first visit to Northern Ireland since the troubles began earlier in the decade.

The climax of the celebrations was a thanksgiving service at St Paul's Cathedral, which the Queen rode to in her Coronation Coach. Among the guests was her 94-year-old great aunt Princess Alice of Athlone who had attended Victoria's Diamond Jubilee in 1897 at the age of fourteen.

Over 100,000 congratulatory letters and cards poured into Buckingham Palace including 3,500 on one day alone. According to her domestic chaplain: "She was floored. She could not believe that people had that much affection for her as a person."

During her Silver Jubilee year the Queen travelled extensively throughout Britain and the Commonwealth.

(Top) On a walkabout following the thanksgiving service in St Paul's Cathedral. June 1977.

(Middle Right) On another walkabout, this time in New Plymouth, New Zealand in February of the same year.

(Bottom Right) Wearing a Maori cloak during the same tour.

(Opposite) A patriotic Pekingese among the flag-waving crowd in Perth, Scotland. May 1977.

(Opposite) A sombre gathering at the funeral of Earl Mountbatten of Burma in Westminster Abbey. The 79-year-old Earl had been murdered by the IRA on Bank Holiday Monday together with his grandson and two others. September 1979.

(Above) A happier day as the Queen and Princess Margaret act as ladies-in-waiting for the Queen Mother as she accepts flowers and cards from well wishers outside Clarence House on her 80th birthday. August 4, 1980.

The following summer the Queen's cousin, Prince Michael of Kent, became the first member of the royal family to marry outside the UK since the Duke of Windsor in 1937. His bride was Baroness Marie-Christine von Reibnitz, a Catholic divorcée. The Pope refused them dispensation to marry in a Catholic church since the Prince announced that their children would be brought up in the Anglican faith. They were married in a Civil Ceremony in Vienna on 30 June 1978. Their son Lord Frederick was born on 6 April 1979 and a daughter, Lady Gabriella, was born two years later.

In August 1979 the Queen was actively involved behind the scenes at the Commonwealth Conference in Lusaka, where a division among Commonwealth leaders over the future government of the former Southern Rhodesia had escalated into a crisis.

Margaret Thatcher, the newly elected British Prime Minister, attending her first such conference, had wondered if the Queen should stay away because of security risks. Elizabeth insisted she should be present at such a critical juncture. She used her strong personal contacts and popularity, especially among the African leaders, to ease tensions and reach an amicable solution – part of which was to regroup again in London for another conference to devise a new constitution for what became known as Zimbabwe.

Later that month, on the morning of 27 August 1979, Elizabeth received the devastating news that Prince Philip's uncle, Earl Mountbatten of Burma, had been assassinated. The Earl was on board his 29 ft fishing boat *Shadow V* off Mullaghmore on the Northern Ireland coast, when the IRA detonated a bomb that had been strapped to the underside of the vessel. His 14-year-old grandson, and a local boat boy, were also killed and the following day, another one of the party, the Dowager Lady Brabourne, died of her injuries.

Buckingham Palace said the Queen was 'deeply shocked' by the atrocity. She and other senior members of the royal family attended the funeral service at Westminster Abbey where Prince Charles read the lesson. For Elizabeth and her family it meant a radical overhaul of royal security, with an inevitably more intense level of protection. The following summer, while out riding with her cousin, Margaret Rhodes, the Queen revealed to her that she had been told the IRA had a special sniper gun that could 'see' through fog.

1980 saw a quartet of special royal birthdays. The Queen Mother was 80, Princess Margaret 50, Princess Anne 30 and Prince Andrew 20.

A thanksgiving service was held at St Paul's Cathedral on 15 July 1980 and the Queen Mother and Prince Charles drove in the 1902 State Landau from Buckingham Palace through packed streets. For once the Queen ceded to her mother the monarch's right to be the last to arrive and first to leave the service. She would do the same later on at the Buckingham Palace balcony appearance and at a gala attended by most of the royal family at Covent Garden, when the Queen and Princess Margaret followed their mother into the royal box.

The Queen Mother's actual birthday was 4 August, and this engendered another outpouring of public affection as the crowds flocked to see her make what was by then a regular birthday appearance at the gates of Clarence House.

That same summer attention turned from the previous queen consort to a possible future one, when Lady Diana Spencer was rumoured to be dating Prince Charles. Years earlier, the prince had said that he felt thirty was the right age to marry and by the late 1970s interest in his love life was a constant theme in the press and gave rise to a new breed of journalist – the freelance photographer – who, rather than being employed by one newspaper, could tout his or her photo scoops to the highest bidder both here and abroad.

Charles, the world's most eligible bachelor, didn't disappoint and gave them a never-ending supply of girlfriends. His first was Lucia Santa Cruz whom he met while a student at Trinity College (and who both he and the Duchess of Cornwall still see whenever she is in the country). His last before Diana was Anna Wallace, who split with the prince in June 1980 after the Windsor Castle ball to celebrate the Queen Mother's birthday. Hurt that the prince had ignored her for most of the evening she reportedly told him "I have never been so badly treated in my life," adding the parting shot, "You've left me alone all evening and now you will have to continue without me."

Other girlfriends included the Duke of Wellington's daughter, Lady Jane Wellesley and Lady Sarah Spencer, Diana's older sister.

Diana, or 'Lady Di' as she soon became known, had been spotted with Charles at Cowes regatta in July and had also been seen watching him play polo at Midhurst in Sussex earlier in the summer. It was when she was photographed watching him fish in the River Dee on the Balmoral estate that she was catapulted into the spotlight. Fleet Street knew the 'Balmoral Test' of meeting the Queen at this most private of residences was always regarded as the litmus test for acceptance into the royal family.

In October the Queen paid a historic visit to the Vatican where, as head of the Church of England, she was received by Pope John Paul II. The same month she paid a more exacting state visit when she toured Morocco. King Hassan insisted on making last minute changes to the itinerary and at one point kept Her Majesty waiting in the desert heat for 30 minutes before he finally turned up for lunch. Sir Philip Moore, then Private Secretary, told reporters, "The Queen has never been so angry."

Back home in the UK, Elizabeth was also unhappy at the media frenzy that had begun after news of Charles and Diana's romance broke that summer. Three months later Diana's mother, Mrs Frances Shand Kydd, complained of the constant press harassment of her daughter and the Queen was angered that her Christmas and New Year break at Sandringham was ruined by having to continually run the gauntlet of long lenses that encircled the estate.

It was while she was staying in Norfolk that winter that the Queen heard the news of the death of her great aunt Princess Alice, Countess of Athlone, at the age of 97 – then a record for royal longevity that would last until the Queen Mother's death at the age of 101. 'Aunt Alice' was Queen Victoria's last surviving granddaughter and was a particular favourite of the Queen's. On her final visit to see the old lady, who by then was bed-ridden in her apartment at Kensington Palace, the monarch was amused when Alice asked her to turn off the electric fire on her way out. "They only put it on because you were coming," said the feisty Victorian.

Seven weeks after Alice's death, on 24 February 1981, the engagement of Charles and Diana was announced. A Buckingham Palace statement said simply: "It is with the greatest pleasure that the Queen and the Duke of Edinburgh announce the betrothal of their beloved son, the Prince of Wales to Lady Diana Spencer, daughter of the Earl Spencer and the Honourable Mrs Shand Kydd."

A month later the Queen gave her formal consent to the marriage at a Privy Council and afterwards posed for photos with her thirty-two year old son and his nineteen year old fiancée.

While preparations for the wedding were well under way, the Queen had a narrow escape from injury when, on 14 June 1981, seventeen-year-old Marcus Sergeant fired six blank shots at her as she rode to Trooping the Colour. Despite riding side saddle the Queen expertly controlled her horse Burmese, who unsurprisingly was spooked by the incident. Her main concern was for the welfare of Philip and Charles who were following her. "I didn't know what was happening," she said later. In September Sergeant was found guilty and jailed for five years, though he was later

Looking resplendent in the customary black floor length dress and veil as she meets Pope John Paul II in the Vatican. The Queen wears the badge and sash of the Order of the Garter together with the royal family orders on her left shoulder. October 17, 1980.

'The stuff of fairy tales' – a balcony kiss for Prince Charles and his twenty year old bride, Lady Diana Spencer on their wedding day. July 29, 1981.

(Opposite) In March of the same year the newly engaged couple pose with the Queen at Buckingham Palace after a Privy Council meeting during which the queen gave her formal consent to the marriage.

committed to a psychiatric hospital.

Six week's later, a record worldwide TV audience of 750 million was reckoned to have tuned in to see Charles and Diana marry at St Paul's Cathedral, in a break with the twentieth century tradition of favouring Westminster Abbey.

It was deemed a State Occasion and nearly every crowned head of Europe was present along with many world leaders. As she emerged from the Glass Coach on to the steps of St Paul's, Diana gave the world its first glimpse of the cream silk gown, designed by David and Elizabeth Emanuel, with its huge 25 yard train especially created to match the grandeur of the setting. In his address following the exchange of vows, the Archbishop of Canterbury, Robert Runcie, memorably said, "this is the stuff of fairy-tales" – a phrase that would come back to haunt the couple in later years as much as Charles's response when asked, on the day of his engagement, if he was in love. "Whatever love means" was his tortured response.

The royal wedding had created a media frenzy that showed no signs of abating throughout the rest of the year.

Following the couple's return from a honeymoon cruise on the Royal Yacht *Britannia* they joined the Queen for a brief holiday on the Balmoral estate. Diana in particular looked tanned and relaxed at a photo call for over a hundred journalists near the River Dee. She told the press pack she could "highly recommend" married life.

Three months later it was announced by Buckingham Palace that Diana was pregnant and that the baby was due the following June. An hour after the news broke, Charles and Diana were at a lunch engagement in the City of London where the prince spoke affectionately about "the overwhelming effect that my dear wife has on everybody."

According to the palace, Elizabeth was 'delighted' with the news. A spokesman added: "The Queen was informed personally by the prince and princess."

As she prepared to enter her fourth decade as sovereign, she did so with the knowledge that not only did she have a new and popular daughter-in-law, but that the birth of this baby, with hopefully others to follow, would guarantee the succession.

The Fairy Queen. Elizabeth II is the epitome of elegance as she arrived for the 1955 Royal Variety Performance at London's Victoria Palace Theatre.

Queen of Style

*The Queen's fashion has been copied
and commented on since she was a small child.*

Children up and down the land wore the same sweaters and woollen dresses teamed with long socks and sandals, or stout winter shoes. Sisters would be dressed identically, like Elizabeth and Margaret, and often wore berets similar to the ones popularised by the princesses.

During the war the two girls followed strict rationing guidelines and had clothing coupons like the rest of the country. They wore simple gingham dresses and quite often Elizabeth's were made from old ones belonging to her mother and then in turn passed on to Margaret.

Elizabeth had little interest in fashion. Her governess Marion Crawford recalled in *The Little Princesses*: "The exact colour of the main garment was given to the tradesman and then the accessories arrived. The Princess was always conservative about her dress and content to wear whatever was laid before her."

For grand state occasions Elizabeth relied on her mother's favourite designer, Norman Hartnell, who created both her wedding dress and her Coronation dress. Hartnell began designing for her at the end of the war and recalled: "she accepted the fitting as part of her official duties, but one did not feel she was interested in clothes as such, or in creating even the latest fashions."

The princess also used one of her mother's milliners, Aage Thaarup, to design her hats, including the ones for her trousseau.

Elizabeth's other main couturier, in her early and middle years, was Hardy Amies. He once said: "She is not a clothes person. She doesn't care. She listens to our advice and then goes off and wears shabby shoes with an outfit because they are comfortable."

Comfort is of course one of her key criteria. The Queen's clothes also have to be bright so she can be seen in a crowd. They mustn't crease and there also has to be arm room so that the Queen can wave and shake hands without danger of ripping the material.

The Queen always pays full price for the outfits she purchases and according to Amies was often taken aback about how much they cost.

Today she has made economies thanks to the skill of her senior dresser Angela Kelly. who succeeded Bobo MacDonald as Elizabeth's personal assistant in the mid-1990s.

These days Angela also designs the clothes and has them made in-house by a team of seamstresses. This also helps the Queen because it makes fittings much easier and more straightforward than having to book sessions with outside designers.

(L-R) Posing in her Norman Hartnell Coronation gown; Wearing a mink coat as she walks to her train at Euston Station, London, en route for Scotland in November 1956; Snugly warm in a leopard-print coat at Sandown Park race course in March 1963; Still elegant at 85 as she arrives for a banquet for Commonwealth leaders in the Pan Pacific Hotel in Perth, western Australia in October 2011.

(L-R) Country Casual. The Queen at the Royal Windsor Horse Show in 2004 and in her riding gear at the same event in 1994. Crowning Glory – hats are an essential part of the Queen's wardrobe. (Top left) At Fishmonger's Hall, London in 1962; (top right) in the pink at a garden party in the grounds of the Royal Hospital, Chelsea, London in 1967; (Bottom left) a striking apple green and white hat for her visit to New Zealand in 1977; (Bottom right) a fake fur hat for the unveiling of a statue of the Queen Mother in The Mall, central London, in 2009.

Off duty the Queen opts for the typical country look, with pleated skirts, Barbour jackets and Pringle cardigans as well as stout leather walking shoes. After Helen Mirren starred as Elizabeth in the movie *The Queen* there was a run on this style, particularly from American fans.

Now in her mid-80s the Queen rigidly maintains the standard of her youth when it comes to fashion. Unlike other royal women she never attends a day-time engagement without her matching hat, coat and dress ensemble, teamed with colour co-ordinated gloves, shoes and bags.

As with so many other aspects of her sixty-year reign, she has remained a credit to herself and the nation.

Members of the Royal Family gather to watch the RAF flypast for the Queen's birthday. June 1984.

New Beginnings

1982 – 1992

*After the success of the Silver Jubilee and
the wedding of Charles and Diana, the Royal Family
began the 1980s very much in the ascendant.*

New Beginnings

After the success of the Silver Jubilee and the wedding of Charles and Diana, the royal family began the 1980s very much in the ascendant.

The focus was increasingly on the younger generation and in particular the new Princess of Wales. Diana was initially shy and reserved but by the middle of the decade had grown in confidence and was developing into a style icon.

Growing alongside her was the media pack. The decade saw the rise of freelance photographers and journalists who would often go to enormous lengths to get an exclusive – and often lucrative – picture or story.

By the 80s the royals had begun to grow adept at using the media themselves and by the middle of the decade several of them were appearing on chat shows and other programmes. In doing so they undoubtedly focused attention on the worthy causes they were involved with; but it came at a price, as some of the mystique of royalty was slowly being eroded.

The Queen's 30th anniversary as monarch occurred against a backdrop of massive press interest in the Princess of Wales.

After the euphoria of the previous year's royal wedding, the Queen and her family had expected the interest in Diana to die down. Instead it grew and grew, thanks to the rivalry between the tabloids and their eagerness to get new angles and stories to satisfy the seemingly insatiable appetite for the latest 'Lady Di' gossip.

The announcement, made in November 1981, that the princess was pregnant only intensified the media interest in the royal couple.

The Queen was concerned about the harassment her daughter-in-law was enduring, and on 8 December summoned Fleet Street's editors to Buckingham Palace for a meeting with her press team, which she would partake in before it finished.

She entered the room as Michael Shea, her Press Secretary, was complaining that Diana could not even pop into the local shops at Tetbury, near Charles's Highgrove estate, without being stalked by photographers.

Although most of the editors were sympathetic, one Sunday tabloid chief cheekily asked the Queen: "Wouldn't it be better to send a servant to the shop for Princess Diana's wine gums". Fixing him with an icy stare, the monarch retorted, "that was a most pompous reply."

At the time of Elizabeth's anniversary in February 1982, the Wales's were on holiday in the Bahamas. A photographer managed to snatch a series of photos of the pregnant princess swimming off a private beach and they made front-page news back in the UK. The Queen called it "a black day for British journalism."

While previous generations of royal mothers had hidden away from view during the latter stages of pregnancy, Diana continued to appear in public right through hers.

She even appeared at Trooping the Colour and the polo at Guard's Club on the Windsor estate the week before having her baby.

Finally at 9:03pm on 21 June 1982 Diana gave birth to Prince William at St Mary's Hospital, Paddington after a long labour. The new prince was the Queen's 3rd grandchild, but significantly he was in direct line to the

The Queen's 30th anniversary as monarch occurred against a backdrop of massive press interest in the Princess of Wales.

The Queen and Prince Philip pose in the grounds of Sandringham House, Norfolk,
to commemorate the 30th anniversary of Her Majesty's accession the throne. February 1982.

(Top) The Queen laughs at Prince Andrew as he bites the stem of a red rose after stepping ashore from the aircraft carrier *HMS Invincible* at Portsmouth Harbour, England. September 17, 1982. The prince had been away for 166 days at sea serving as a helicopter pilot during the Falklands War.

(Bottom Right) Ronald Reagan enjoyed riding as much as the Queen does and it was only natural that the two of them should tour the Home Park at Windsor on horseback during the US President's visit to Britain. June 1982.

(Bottom Left) The Queen bids farewell to Pope John Paul II at Buckingham Palace during his pastoral visit to Britain. May 1982.

(Opposite) Four generations of the royal family gather at Buckingham Palace for the christening of Prince William on August 4 1982, the Queen Mother's 82nd birthday.

throne and in the fullness of time would succeed Charles III as king.

The Queen called in to see the new addition to the family and joked: "Well at least he hasn't got his father's ears!"

During that spring Britain had been involved in the ten week Falklands conflict. The Queen's concerns were threefold – politically as Head of State; militarily as Head of the Armed Forces and personally as the mother of a serving helicopter pilot, Prince Andrew.

The prince was part of the naval task force sent by the British Prime Minister, Margaret Thatcher, to take back control of the Falkland Islands. These had been invaded on 2 April 1982 by Argentina in a dispute over sovereignty.

The war lasted 74 days and claimed the lives of 257 British and 649 Argentine service personnel.

Prince Andrew played an active part in the fighting. He used his helicopter as a decoy for Exocet missiles and helped rescue the crew of the bombed *Atlantic Conveyor* ship. He later recalled: "It was horrific and terrible and something I'll never forget. It was probably my most

frightening moment of the war."

The Queen sailed out from port to meet Andrew on board *HMS Invincible* on his return to Portsmouth on 16 September after over five months away at sea.

While conflict raged in the South Atlantic, it was business as usual for the Queen who greeted two widely different heads of state. In May, Pope John Paul II paid a pastoral visit to the UK – the first by a Pope to Britain for 450 years. During his tour he drove through the gates of Buckingham Palace in his 'Popemobile' before spending 35 minutes in talks with the Queen, Elizabeth II, the supreme governor of the Church of England. As he prepared to take his leave, he warmly shook the Queen's hand and told her: "I will pray for your son in the Falklands."

The following month the US President, Ronald Reagan, and his wife Nancy stayed with the Queen at Windsor Castle, where the two horse-loving leaders enjoyed an early morning ride in Windsor Great Park. In 1983 the Reagans returned the favour and invited the Queen to their ranch in California, a visit best remembered now for the storms

which bashed the coast of West America, making the journey to the mountaintop retreat hazardous.

On 9 July 1982 the Queen was directly involved in a major lapse of security when Michael Fagan, an unemployed north London labourer, not only managed to break into Buckingham Palace but then made his way to the Queen's bedroom unimpeded, and spent ten minutes alone with Her Majesty.

The incident happened at 7:15am, and at first the Queen thought it was her maid about to wake her with her early morning tea. Instead it was Fagan who awoke the monarch. Elizabeth twice rang the panic button to the police lodge for help, but to no avail. According to the intruder the Queen did not appear nervous or worried. And when he asked for a cigarette she cleverly used this as an excuse to get him out into the corridor. Here they were confronted by a maid with a Hoover who exclaimed: "Bloody 'ell, Ma'am, what's he doing here." At this point the Queen's page, Paul Whybrew, returned from walking the corgis and kept Fagan occupied by offering him a drink while the Queen

waited for the police to finally arrive on the scene.

Initially the incident was hushed up but the ensuing Home Office investigation was leaked to the press. Fagan himself said the royal security was "diabolical" and the Queen, for one, could hardly disagree.

The 1980s saw a gradual deterioration between the palace and the press. The latter had always been reassured by the fact that traditionally the Queen can't answer back, but increasingly the monarch sought legal redress for the more extreme examples of intrusion and harassment.

In February 1983 she imposed an injunction on a former palace servant for revealing royal secrets. This followed revelations in *The Sun* about the alleged behaviour of Prince Andrew and his then girlfriend, Koo Stark, under the headline "Queen Koo's Romps at the Palace."

Four years later the Queen once again initiated proceedings against the media for breach of copyright when *The Sun* published a private letter written by the Duke of Edinburgh to the Commandant of the Royal Marines in which he refers to Prince Edward's decision to

A giant screen displaying a portrait of the Queen at the Queen Elizabeth II Jubilee Sports Centre during the closing ceremony of the 1982 Commonwealth Games in Brisbane Australia.

(Inset) The Queen congratulates athletes during a medal ceremony during the games.

(Opposite) One for the album. The Queen takes photos with her Leica camera during her visit to the South Sea Islands of Tuvalu. October 1982.

(Top) A dramatic entrance. The Queen arrives through the avenues of guns during the second day of her review of the Royal Regiment of Artillery at Dortmund in what was then called East Germany. May 23, 1984.

(Bottom Left) With the proprietor Rupert Murdoch (left) at *The Times* newspaper building at Grays Inn Road, London, during a visit to mark the paper's bicentenary. February 1985.

(Bottom right) Holding a traditional straw pocketbook given her by well-wisher as she toured the famed straw market in Nassau, capitol of the Bahamas. October 12, 1985.

quit his service career with the unit. The following year the same newspaper agreed to pay £100,000 to charity after publishing a private photo of the Queen and her newborn granddaughter, Princess Beatrice, taken at Balmoral during the summer.

One positive outcome of the decade for the royal family was the increased recognition of the work carried out by both Prince Charles and Princess Anne.

Anne had an initially rocky start to public life. She once said: "they tried to make me out to be the fairytale princess and that didn't work." She was known as 'Princess Sourpuss' and noted for telling photographers to "Naff Off" and worse.

Finally she found her milieu in her capacity as President of the Save the Children Fund. In the autumn of 1982 Princess Anne undertook a gruelling six-nation tour of Africa and the Middle East on behalf of the STCF. Never cut out for attending flower shows and garden parties, Anne thrived on driving along dusty roads in a Landrover to reach isolated communities which her charity was trying to help. Newspaper editors changed their stance and began to compliment her for her hands-on approach during her 14,000 mile tour, in which she saw starving children in refugee camps in Somalia and visited makeshift hospitals in Beirut and Swaziland.

Two months after the Live Aid concert helped to raise millions for Africa's starving populations, Anne made a crusading speech to a conference of 60 Third World countries in Inverness. "Drought and famine are not new in Africa," she told them. "Their effect can be moderated with sensible and basic precautions and planning by everybody."

In June 1987, Anne finally gave into pressure from her family and accepted the Queen's offer of the title Princess Royal. This courtesy title is bestowed on the eldest daughter of the sovereign shortly after the death of the previous holder. This time there was a 22 year gap between the death of the Queen's aunt, Princess Mary, in 1965 and Anne's acceptance of the honour.

Prince Charles also proved he was not going to let his royal status impede his desire to speak on a wide variety of sometimes contentious issues. In May 1984, he addressed a gathering of leading architects at Hampton Court. He launched an attack on the work of modern architects and in particular those who had submitted plans for the proposed extension of the National Gallery. He memorably caused a rumpus in the press by singling out the design by Peter Ahrends as "a kind of vast municipal fire station …like a monstrous carbuncle on the face of a much loved and elegant friend."

Besides architecture he was also concerned with race relations and the problems facing multi-faith Britain. His critics picked up on the fact that many of his opinions were diametrically opposed to those of Margaret Thatcher and her cabinet.

Stories circulated in the mid-80s that the Queen herself was concerned at Mrs Thatcher's radical reforms which she was said to find 'uncaring, confrontational and divisive.' The story made headline news in July 1986 in what it called an 'unprecedented disclosure of the Monarch's political views.' *The Sunday Times* carried the story that the Queen, like her son, was profoundly worried about the direction in which the country was heading. The reports were made all the more sensational because Elizabeth has always steered a remarkably non-political course through her long reign.

The source of the leak was discovered to be the palace Press Secretary, Michael Shea, who immediately denied the Queen had ever said anything along these lines. Her Private Secretary, William Heseltine, fired off a letter to *The Times* in which he stated that it was "preposterous" that the Queen, after thirty-four years on the throne, would suddenly abandon her strict rule on unbiased impartiality and attack the government of the day.

In 1986 the nation geared up for the second major royal wedding of the decade when it was announced Prince Andrew was to marry Sarah Ferguson. 'Fergie', as the press dubbed her, was widely regarded at the time as the perfect choice for Andrew. She had impeccable pedigree. She was not only descended from Charles II but her maternal grandmother was a cousin of the Queen's aunt, Princess Alice, Duchess of Gloucester. Her father, 'Major Ron', was

a polo-playing friend of Prince Philip's and was Prince Charles's honorary Polo Manager.

In January 1986 the Queen invited Sarah to Sandringham where the royal family welcomed the ebullient, fun-loving and confident young lady. Elizabeth took to her straightaway and found her much easier to deal with than the complicated and insecure Diana.

Andrew and Sarah became engaged on 19 March and were married on 23 July. The Queen created her son Duke of York, a title particularly close to her heart as it had been the one bestowed on her father in 1920 and she herself had been Princess Elizabeth of York. As a wedding present Elizabeth paid the £3.5 million cost of building the couple a dream house at Sunninghill near to Windsor Castle. The sprawling, ranch style house was immediately dubbed 'South York' after the Southfork estate owned by the oil-rich Ewing family in the TV show *Dallas*.

That same spring marked the final chapter of another royal romance when the ailing Duchess of Windsor died in her Paris home at the age of 89. The Queen had only met her aunt on a handful of occasions. In deference to her mother she had always kept the Windsors at arms length and they were never invited to any family events other than the plaque unveiling to mark Queen Mary's 100th birthday in 1967. At the Duchess's funeral in St George's Chapel, Windsor, it was noted that Wallis's name was not even mentioned. Later, however, it was noted that away from all but a few family members and close friends, Elizabeth had tears in her eyes as Wallis's body was placed in the ground next to her husband's in the private burial ground at Frogmore.

On 8 August 1988 at 8:18pm the Duchess of York gave birth to a baby girl, the Queen's fifth grandchild at London's Portland Hospital. In keeping with tradition a copy of the bulletin was fixed to the gates of Buckingham Palace and the following day a 41-gun salute was fired from both Hyde Park and Tower Green. The baby was baptised Beatrice Elizabeth Mary at the Chapel Royal, St James's Palace, on 20 December.

The Queen undertook several memorable tours during

In June 1986, the Queen rides her horse Burmese for the final time during the Trooping of the Colour in London. The mare was a gift from the Royal Canadian Mounted Police in 1969 and the Queen rode her to the Trooping for eighteen consecutive years.

(Opposite) The royal family on the balcony of Buckingham Palace following the wedding of Prince Andrew to Sarah Ferguson. On the morning of the wedding it was announced that the Queen had given her second son the title of Duke of York. July 23, 1986.

The Queen and Duke pose on the Great Wall of China at the Bedaling Pass, 50 miles north-west of Beijing, on the third day of their State Visit to the country. (Inset) Presenting the Order of Merit to Mother Teresa at the Presidential Palace in Delhi, India. November 1983.

(Opposite) During her 1983 visit to Kenya, the Queen visited the site of the original Treetops hotel where she was staying when her father died. The new hotel is the background. It was the Queen's first visit to the East African country since 1952.

the decade. In 1983 she visited India and awarded Mother Teresa the prestigious Order of Merit. The order is the sole gift of the monarch and is held by only 24 people at one time. The same year the Queen visited Kenya and in a poignant visit saw the new Treetops Hotel on the site where she became Queen in 1952.

One of the most historic tours of her reign was her week long visit to China in October 1986 - the first by a reigning British monarch. Besides the usual state banquets and meetings with political figures there was also time for sightseeing. They toured the Great Wall, posing for photographers before setting off for a short walk along one of its sections allowing the Queen to take her own snaps. They also travelled to Xi'an in the Shaanxi province to see the Terracotta Army that had been unearthed only twelve years earlier.

The China tour was overshadowed by a diplomatic incident when the Duke of Edinburgh came out with one of his legendary gaffes, telling British students at a reception that he found Beijing "ghastly" and joking that "if you stay here much longer you'll go back with slitty eyes." While press secretary Michael Shea insisted: "Jocular comments have been taken completely out of context," the British press, relishing a good news story, labelled the prince "the Great Wally of China."

While Charles and Anne had grown in public esteem during the decade, neither Andrew nor his younger brother Edward captured the public's imagination in the same way. Despite the success of his naval career, his service in the Falklands conflict, his marriage and the birth of his daughter Beatrice in 1988, Andrew never gained the same level of respect enjoyed by his parents, grandmother or other working royals.

His 1984 five-day tour of America was a PR disaster after he took a spray gun from a painter during a visit to a housing estate in Los Angeles, and sprayed white paint over photographers and their expensive cameras. Although he made a belated apology, Andrew's visit was widely believed to have harmed the royal family's image in the United States. One commentator labelled it "the most unpleasant

During the 1980s the Royals invaded their own privacy by appearing regularly on TV and radio.

royal visit since they burnt the White House in 1812."

Prince Edward also failed to attract much sympathy when in January 1987 he quit the marines. The prince's resignation, after just four months training, was a blow to Prince Philip who is the Marines' honorary Captain General and who was said to be furious at his son's decision.

The dilemma for Andrew and Edward has always been that there is no obvious role for the sovereign's younger children other than charity work. Edward tried his hand at theatre work and was invited to join Andrew Lloyd Webber's *Really Useful Theatre Company*, which led him on to found his own TV production company with decidedly mixed fortunes.

During the 1980s the royals invaded their own privacy by appearing regularly on TV and radio. Princess Anne, the Duke of York and their father appeared on shows like *Aspel*, *Wogan* and *Parkinson* and Anne also made a memorable appearance on *A Question of Sport*. Even Princess Margaret, normally a stickler for protocol and tradition, appeared on *The Archers* playing herself on an NSPCC visit, and was also a guest on *Desert Island Discs*.

These royal appearances reached their lowest point in June 1987 when Prince Edward produced *It's a Royal Knockout* as a charity fundraiser that rapidly turned into a PR disaster. Edward, Andrew, Sarah, and, most surprisingly, Anne agreed to captain four teams of celebrities who competed in games at Alton Towers to raise money. To make matters worse, Prince Edward stormed out of a post-production press conference. After asking the media what they thought about the reaction to the show the prince received a lukewarm response, prompting him to snap, "well thanks a lot", before walking out on them. The Queen's reaction was never made public, though it can easily be guessed.

While Charles and Diana never took part in any of the above they were rapidly becoming their own soap opera with every twist and turn of their marriage making newspaper headlines.

In October 1985, 20 million UK viewers watched a deferential 45-minute interview with the Prince and Princess of Wales by veteran broadcaster, Alastair Burnett. Diana told him her most important role: "is supporting my husband whenever I can and always being behind him and also, most important, being a wife and mother."

Behind the scenes it was another matter, but it only became apparent in the next decade, that both the prince and princess were seeing other people by the mid to late 80s.

Princess Anne's marriage was also in trouble. In April 1989 Scotland Yard launched a top-level investigation to find the thief who stole four letters sent to the Princess Royal by the Queen's equerry, Commander Timothy Laurence, which were said to be "tender and affectionate." The affair prompted speculation that the princess's fifteen-year marriage to Mark Phillips was in trouble. Finally on 30 August, Buckingham Palace announced that Anne and Mark were to separate, though there were no plans to divorce.

For the Queen, the 1980s ended on a sad note. To her former private secretary, Martin Charteris, she remarked: "And I thought I had brought them up so well." Later she poignantly asked a lady-in-waiting, "where did we go wrong?"

On 23 March 1990, the Duchess of York gave birth to her second daughter at 7:58pm, again at the Portland Hospital. This was the Queen's sixth grandchild and she was said to be 'delighted' while Prince Andrew, who was present during the caesarean birth said "the

Diana told him her most important role: "is supporting my husband whenever I can and always being behind him and also, most important, being a wife and mother."

(Top) The Queen Mother poses with her family outside Clarence House, her London home, on her ninetieth birthday. August 4, 1990.

(Bottom) The Queen is never happier than when she is at the races. Here she shows her excitement as she watches Willie Carson cross the finishing line on Hashwan at the 1989 Epsom Derby with her private secretary, Sir William Heseltine. shows her excitement at the Epsom horserace meeting on Wednesday. June 7, 1989.

The 'Queen Mum' as she was affectionately known celebrated her 90th birthday on 4 August on what turned out to be one of the hottest summer days ever recorded.

baby is lovely." Surprisingly she wasn't baptised until the following Christmas-time when the royal family had gathered together at Sandringham as usual. 'Fergie' has long been fascinated by Victorian history. She named her new daughter Eugenie (after the Empress of the French), Victoria (after the Queen) and Helena (after Victoria's third daughter).

Also in March, Viscount Linley, the Queen's nephew, won a high court case for libel. He was awarded £5,000 in civil damages and £30,000 in punitive damages against the *Today* newspaper over allegations he poured lager over customers in a Chelsea pub. It suggested a new tough line was being adopted against the media by those close to the Queen.

Four months later the palace won a ban on the publication of a book of behind-the-scenes revelations written by a former member of staff. The Queen's solicitors said Malcolm Barker, a former clerk, had breached a confidentiality agreement he signed in 1980.

The Queen watched political events in East Europe with a keen eye during the momentous days of the late 80s and early 90s. Several members of her family were early visitors to the former eastern bloc countries. On 7 May 1990 Charles and Diana arrived in Budapest, just months after Hungary ended forty years of Communist rule. They were the first British royals to visit since the war. It was clearly an emotional moment for President Goncz's wife, Zsuzsa, who could be seen dabbing her eyes and holding Diana's hand as they walked along the guard of honour.

The same month, the Princess Royal visited Moscow, and ended a 72-year rift between the British royal family and the Soviet Union, by shaking hands with President Mikhail Gorbachev. Anne had visited the country before,

but in her capacity as an equestrian competitor. During her 17-day stay she visited many areas of the country including peasant villages in Siberia and farms near Kiev. Her visit was widely regarded as a precursor to one by the Queen, who Gorbachev had invited to his country when he met her at Windsor Castle in April 1989.

Finally there was another historic moment, when in March 1990 the Queen Mother made a private visit to see the Berlin Wall, which was still standing at the time, but shorn of its colourful graffiti by souvenir hunters. The royal matriarch, once dubbed 'the most dangerous woman in Europe' by Hitler, because of her brilliant PR skills that rallied the British during the war, posed happily in front of the structure and was handed pieces of it to take home as a souvenir.

The 'Queen Mum', as she was affectionately known, celebrated her 90th birthday on 4 August on what turned out to be one of the hottest summer days ever recorded. She appeared at the gates of Clarence House with all her family before enjoying a celebratory lunch party and a trip to Covent Garden to watch the Royal Ballet.

Three days earlier she had been on a nostalgic trip to the east end of London, which she had memorably visited several times at the height of the Blitz. Fifty years on she recalled what she said were "the dark days of the war" and told locals, "It's good to be back."

On 28th November 1990 John Major went to Buckingham Palace to kiss hands as the Queen's ninth Prime Minister, following the unexpected collapse of Margaret Thatcher's government after eleven years in power.

The Queen has never revealed which of her Prime Ministers she does and does not get on with, but her relationship with Margaret Thatcher has been described as

everything from 'formal' to 'rigid'. The two never had the same rapport she had with, for example, Harold Wilson or Alec Douglas Hume.

Both women were discreet about their discussions. "Mrs Thatcher never spoke about her meetings at the palace," recalled one aide, "and never spoke about the Queen, except in the most dutiful terms."

Nevertheless following her retirement they have maintained cordial relations and the Queen looked happy and relaxed at both Thatcher's 70th and 80th birthday parties.

The last year of the Queen's fourth decade as monarch began with British involvement in the Gulf War, and criticism about royal reaction to it.

On 22 December 1990, Prince Charles visited Saudi Arabia to inspect British Troops preparing for possible action against Iraq if the latter failed to withdraw from Kuwait. UK service personnel had been in the area since September as part of Operation Desert Shield with the USA and France.

Action began with aerial bombardment on 16 January, followed by a ground offensive a week later. Meanwhile, at home, newspapers criticised younger members of the royal family in particular for not setting a better example at a time of war. The stories were initially spun by the tabloids but were soon picked up by the broadsheets. *The Sunday Times* criticised some of the Queen's relatives for their fun-loving lifestyle and lamented the fact that none of them were on active service, with the exception of Prince Andrew, whose ship was nowhere near the Gulf. *The Guardian* weighed in with stories of royal partying and "Fergie spending £5 million on a house that's always empty."

The Sun claimed that the Queen had told her family to avoid any frivolity and the palace revealed Her Majesty was in close touch with the government over the war and had been given a series of briefings from the military to keep her abreast of developments.

It was the first time the monarchy had been attacked for its behaviour during wartime. A generation later and, perhaps, lessons have been learned since the active service

The Queen attending 1989 Royal Variety Performance at the London Palladium.

(Opposite) Greeting Prime Minister Margaret Thatcher as she arrives for dinner aboard the Royal Yacht *Britannia*, in Kuala Lumpur. October 1989.

Dubbed 'the talking hat' – this moment on the Queen's 1991 visit to the USA occurred when aides forgot to adjust the podium before the royal visitor addressed dignitaries on the South Lawn of the White House watched by President George Bush Snr.

(Opposite) Two days later the Queen was applauded when, before addressing the US Congress she joked, "I do hope you can all see me." Vice President Dan Quayle and House Speaker Thomas Foley enjoy the moment.

of Prince Harry in Afghanistan and the close involvement of members of the royal forces in supporting the military is only too clear.

In May 1991, in the final months of her fourth decade, Elizabeth visited the United States. She became the first British Head of State to address a joint meeting of the US Congress in Washington. Her deadpan comment: "I do hope you can all see me this time" – a reference to her White House arrival speech when someone failed to adjust the podium so her face was blocked by microphones – won her a standing ovation.

During her speech she talked of the special relationship between the two countries and thanked Americans for "their steadfast loyalty to our common enterprise throughout this turbulent century."

Her speech showed her continued mastery of diplomacy, as her biographer Ben Pimlott noted: "It was a curiously triumphant moment, which a mere Prime Minister – or elected figurehead – might have found it hard to capture."

However it was events far more personal and closer to home that would dominate the Queen's fifth decade.

Royal Homes

*From weekdays at the palace to weekends at Windsor, from Christmas
at Sandringham to summer at Balmoral, the Queen's year is divided between
her official and private homes.*

Buckingham Palace

Buckingham Palace is the Queen's official London residence. She and the Duke live in private apartments on the north side, overlooking Green Park. Princes Andrew and Edward also have rooms here in what used to be the royal nursery. In total the palace has 19 state rooms, 52 royal and guest bedrooms, 188 staff bedrooms, 92 offices, 78 bathrooms and lavatories and an extensive basement. Probably its best-known feature is the balcony, part of the East Front, which was a Victorian addition.

Windsor Castle

Said to be the Queen's favourite home, Windsor Castle is where she spent most of the Second World War. Today she lives in apartments overlooking the East Terrace and for most of the year she spends her weekends here, walking her dogs and still enjoying a morning ride in the Home Park.

Sandringham House

Sandringham was built by the Queen's great grandfather, Edward VII, when he was Prince of Wales, in the 1860s. Along with Balmoral it is the private property of the monarch and when Edward VIII abdicated in 1936 he sold them for £1 million to the Queen's father, George VI. Members of the royal family spend Christmas and New Year here.

Balmoral Castle

Queen Victoria fell in love with the Scottish Highlands and she and Prince Albert built Balmoral on the site of an older castle next to the River Dee. The present Queen spends about ten weeks there each summer and she enjoys walking, riding and regular barbecues on the estate. Prince Charles stays at nearby Birkhall several times a year and the Queen gave princes William and Harry a cottage called *Tam-na-Ghar*.

Palace of Holyroodhouse

This is the Queen's official residence in Scotland and she usually stays here for a week in late June or early July. It stands in the heart of Edinburgh, at the foot of the Royal Mile. In September 2010 Elizabeth hosted a reception here for Pope Benedict XVI during his visit to the UK and in July 2011 she also gave a wedding reception at Holyroodhouse for granddaughter Zara Phillips and Mike Tindall.

St James's Palace

The palace was built between 1532 and 1540 by Henry VIII on the site of the Hospital of St James. For three hundred years it was lived in by the monarch until Victoria moved to Buckingham Palace. It is still the 'Court' that ambassadors and high commissioners are accredited to. It also houses royal offices including those of princes William and Harry. In 1997 the body of Diana, Princess of Wales, lay here in the Chapel Royal before her funeral.

Clarence House

This was built in the 1820s for the Duke of Clarence, later King William IV. It was later the home of Queen Victoria's mother, the Duchess of Kent. After the Second World War it was refurbished for Princess Elizabeth and Prince Philip and they lived here from 1949 until 1953, the year after her accession. It then became the London residence of the Queen Mother until her death in 2002, when it was given to the Prince of Wales.

Kensington Palace

Originally called Nottingham House, this was bought by William III in 1689 and extended by Sir Christopher Wren. Queen Victoria was born here in 1819 and Elizabeth II's grandmother, Princess Mary of Teck, was also born here in 1867. It was the childhood home of princes William and Harry. William now lives here with his wife Catherine, in Nottingham Cottage, part of the rambling estate, and they will move into Princess Margaret's former apartment, No 1a Kensington Palace, after it has been restored.

Queen Elizabeth II and the Duke of Edingburgh at the Guildhall, London, where they attended a luncheon hosted by the Corporation of London to mark the 40th anniversary of her accession.

Darker Days

1992 – 2002

For the royal family, the 1990s
turned out to be the most traumatic
decade of the Queen's reign.

Darker Days

With the marriages of three of her four children ending in divorce, a major fire at Windsor Castle, growing disquiet about the tax free status of the sovereign at a time of economic gloom and, most cataclysmic of all, the death of Diana, Princess of Wales, this was a dark decade.

The year 1992 opened on an upbeat note. 6 February 1992 marked the 40th anniversary of Her Majesty's accession. There were no plans for an official public celebration and the Queen vetoed, on the grounds of cost, the suggestion that a fountain should be erected in Parliament Square to mark the event.

There were also no plans for an Abdication. The previous autumn a rumour began to spread that the Queen would step down as monarch on her 40th anniversary and that she might announce this in her Christmas Broadcast at the end of 1991.

Instead the Queen used the speech to firmly emphasise her commitment to her role as well as her hope to serve Britain and the Commonwealth "for some years to come."

On the actual anniversary the Queen visited Tapping House, a hospice at Snettisham, near her Sandringham estate. It was a poignant reminder that her father had died of cancer at Sandringham in the days before people fully realised the connection between heavy smoking and the disease.

Newspapers used the anniversary to acknowledge the Queen's continuing contribution to the life of the country. *The Observer* stated it would be hard not to respect "this level-headed, devoted, plain-speaking, commonsensical woman who inspires affection."

The Queen had agreed to co-operate on a landmark documentary to mark her 40th year as monarch. The 1969 film *Royal Family* had looked to the future and used the Queen's working life to examine the role that Charles would one day take on. *Elizabeth R* concentrated very much on the monarch herself.

Edward Mirzoeff, the documentary's producer, said at the time: "You're always aware exactly who she is. There's inevitably a certain remoteness about her. She never gives interviews, and you can't film her eating or drinking. Throughout our year of filming, I saw over and over again how all kinds of people are completely overwhelmed by her."

Although the Queen has never been interviewed by anyone in the media, she did agree to contribute a voice over. Talking of her role as monarch she says: "In this existence, the job and the life go together – you can't really divide it up."

Of her Prime Ministers she reveals: "they unburden themselves if they have any problems... occasionally one can put one's point of view and perhaps they hadn't seen it from that angle." She never of course revealed who unburdened themselves and why; one of her strengths as a constitutional monarch has been her total discretion. She is the original 'keeper of secrets.'

In retrospect one of the most telling comments relates to her concerns about the next generation's ability to cope with the demands of royal life. "I think that this is what the younger members find difficult," she says "the regimented side."

The year 1992 opened on an upbeat note. 6 February marked the 40th anniversary of Her Majesty's accession.

The Queen watches a performance of *The Royal Kitchen Mice Polka* by the Youth Ballet as part of a tribute to celebrate the 40th anniversary of the Queen's accession, at Fountain Court, Hampton Court Palace. July 1992.

(Top Left) Arriving at Spencer House in London to attend a dinner hosted by the Prime Minister John Major and former PMs to mark the 40th anniversary of her accession. July 1992.

(Top Right) Attending a gala dinner hosted by President Francois Mitterrand at the Elysee Palace in Paris during her third State Visit to France. June 1992.

(Left) The royal couple are clearly enjoying the Great Event a celebration of the Queen's forty years on the throne held at Earl's Court, London. October 1992.

Her fears were justified since even before the documentary had been shown the strong royal family unit slowly had begun to dismantle in a whole series of personal crises.

On 15 January 1992 photos of the Duchess of York and her Texan oil millionaire friend, Steve Wyatt, surfaced in a tabloid newspaper. Prince Andrew was said to be particularly upset at the snaps that showed Wyatt with Princess Beatrice, which looked as if he was usurping the Duke's paternal role.

It was the latest in a series of PR disasters featuring Fergie, gleefully reported on by the press, and about which the palace were growing increasingly impatient.

The following week the Yorks decided to separate. In her memoirs Sarah recalls going to Sandringham on the 22 January to tell the Queen. Walking in, clutching her rosary for strength, she told her mother-in-law: "I am so sorry but I think this is best for you and your family - I can't go on letting you down."

According to Sarah: "The Queen looked sadder than I had ever seen her. She asked me to reconsider, to be strong and go forward."

On 16 March 1992, the Queen dissolved parliament and a general election was called for later in the spring. On the same day it was announced that the Yorks would separate.

It was a great blow for the Queen who had formed a much stronger bond with Sarah than she had ever had with Diana. The two went riding together at Windsor and enjoyed nights out at the theatre – in February 1988, for instance, the Duchess accompanied the Queen to see Maggie Smith in *Lettice and Lovage* at the Globe Theatre.

Worse was to come later in the year. Sarah had remained on cordial terms with her royal in-laws and was invited to stay with them at Balmoral in August. While she was there, the *Daily Mirror* published snooped photos of the topless Duchess having her toes sucked by another friend, John Bryan, in full view of the young princesses.

Sarah was devastated and the royal family mortified. "What do you all do?" Princess Margaret told a friend later, "We all had to come down to breakfast anyway." A few days later a forlorn Sarah was snapped leaving the estate en route to Aberdeen airport.

After four years of official separation the Yorks announced their decision to divorce in 1996.

Meanwhile Sarah's sister-in-law, the Princess of Wales, was about to inflict an even greater bombshell. Rumours that all was not well in the Wales's marriage had been circulating since the late 1980s. They grew in 1991 when the tabloids revealed that Prince Charles was not planning anything to celebrate Diana's 30th birthday on 1 July. The truth was that he'd asked her and she had declined the offer of a party or anything else to mark the occasion.

According to royal biographer Robert Lacey, the series of marital squabbles over the birthday was the trigger that brought Diana to co-operate, via friends, with a new biography of the princess by Andrew Morton.

Lacey writes: "The turning point in the history of the modern British monarchy occurred in a transport café in North Ruislip in the summer of 1991."

James Colthurst, an old Etonian friend of Diana's, met Morton and agreed to act as a go-between for author and subject. The princess would record tapes outlining her grievances about her marriage and life in the royal family and Colthurst would feed back Morton's questions and requests for clarification.

Having a friend as an intermediary allowed Diana to honestly say she had not met Morton when he was writing the book. The full story of her co-operation only emerged following her death.

Meanwhile, in February 1992, the couple undertook a strained tour of India, during which the princess memorably posed alone on a marble seat as she stared wistfully at that great monument to love, the Taj Mahal. In Jaipur she made another point by turning her head when Charles kissed her cheek as she presented him with a cup after a polo match. As the prince awkwardly kissed the side of her neck it was a clear sign to the assembled journalists that the marriage, like the kiss, was completely askew.

The Morton book *Diana: Her True Story* was serialised in *The Sunday Times*, beginning on 7 June 1992, and its impact stunned the royal family and their advisers.

Readers were told that after a row with Charles the princess had thrown herself down the wooden staircase at Sandringham while she was pregnant with William. There were stories of her attempts to slash her wrists with a razor and her visits to a succession of therapists. Also, for the first time, the world was made aware that Charles had resumed his affair with one of his early flames, Camilla Parker Bowles.

The timing couldn't have been worse for the Queen and her family. The following week was Trooping the Colour, followed by the Garter Ceremony at Windsor and four days of Royal Ascot – all high profile events that ordinarily attract a media scrum, but that year the press interest went off the scale.

The Queen carried on dutifully as ever, with little outward sign of the effect the biography had made on her. Diana continued to take centre stage, sharing a carriage with the Queen Mother at the Trooping and appearing at the Garter and Ascot.

When Robert Fellowes, the Queen's Private Secretary and Diana's brother-in-law, asked the princess if she had co-operated with Morton she flatly denied she had. Two days later, however, she was photographed leaving the Fulham home of her friend Carolyn Bartholomew, who had been one of the named sources in the book. The message was clear that Diana either was involved with the book or at least approved it.

Before the book came out the Queen and Duke had invited Charles and Diana for a summit meeting to try to talk through the problems, explaining to the younger couple how all marriages go through problem patches and that they were willing to help. Philip asked: "Can you tell us what's the matter, Diana?" but the princess collapsed in tears. Charles was asked the same question and would only respond: "What, and read it all in the newspapers tomorrow? No thank you," a reference to his wife's habit of frequently leaking stories to trusted journalists.

The deterioration of the Wales's marriage fuelled the tabloid war that had started with the Fergie toe-sucking scandal. In August *The Sun* released the transcript of a tape it had been hanging onto for three years that purported

(Above) Although the marriage of Charles and Diana was spiralling out of control during 1992, particularly after the publication of *Diana: Her True Story* by Andrew Morton, the Queen and Queen Mother did their best to include the princess at royal events.

(Above) Diana and the Queen Mother share a carriage during the procession to Royal Ascot in June.

(Right) Diana has a front row seat at the Great Event, a celebration of the 40th anniversary of the Queen's accession, held at London's Earl Court. October 26, 1992.

(Opposite) Diana still holding centre stage at the Trooping the Colour, June 1992.

The forlorn figure of the Queen surveys the fire damage to Windsor Castle, which started the previous day, which was her 45th wedding anniversary.

(Opposite) A few days later the Queen delivers a speech after a Guildhall luncheon to mark the 40th anniversary of her accession to the throne. In the speech she branded 1992 her 'Annus Horribilis' due to criticisms of the Royal family.

to be a conversation between Diana and another friend, James Gilbey. The latter referred to her as 'Squidge' or 'Squidgy' and listened as she poured out her feelings about the royal family.

Inevitably dubbed 'Squidgygate' the scandal was followed by a similar one in November when the transcript of an alleged taped conversation between Prince Charles and his lover, emerged in *The Mirror* and was duly labelled 'Camillagate.'

For the Queen, the year went from bad to worse. On 20 November, her 45th wedding anniversary, a fire broke out at Windsor Castle when a spotlight ignited a curtain in the private chapel in the north-east part of the castle.

Fire quickly spread through the State Apartments, completely gutting the historic St George's Hall. Fortunately most of the treasures had already been removed as a complete electrical rewiring was being undertaken. In the end only one painting and a large piece of furniture were lost, but the damage to the fabric of the building was extensive.

Prince Andrew who was on hand to help evacuate carpets and other fittings, told an impromptu press conference that his mother was "shocked and devastated." Prince Philip, who was at a conference in Argentina, spent hours on the phone trying to console her. Later the Queen travelled to see the damage for herself, looking distressed as smoke still poured out of the Brunswick Tower above the seat of the fire.

Initial sympathy for the Queen was reduced when the Heritage Secretary, Peter Brooke, glibly announced that the castle was uninsured and that the Government would pay the repair bill – estimated at between £20 and £40 million – from the public purse.

A few days later the Queen addressed the great and good at a banquet in London's Guildhall to mark her 40th anniversary. "Nineteen ninety-two is not a year I shall look back on with undiluted pleasure," she told them in a voice

hoarse from having inhaled the smoke from the burning castle. She went on to describe the year as an 'Annus Horribilis.'

December was a month with more mixed fortunes. On the 9th it was announced that Charles and Diana would separate. In the House of Commons the Prime Minister, John Major, broke the news to MPs but insisted there was no question of divorce and that should Charles become King, Diana would automatically become Queen.

On a happier note, three days later, Princess Anne married her mother's former equerry, Commander Tim Laurence, at Crathie Kirk on Deeside, with daughter Zara as bridesmaid and her parents, brother Andrew and the Queen Mother also present. Unsurprisingly Charles and Diana stayed away.

The royal finances were a continuing theme during the early 1990s. On 26 November 1992, John Major announced in the Commons that in the following year the Queen and Prince Charles would start paying tax on their private income.

The initiative had come from the palace at the beginning of the 1992 and was due to be implemented in 1993 anyway, but the public disquiet over the possibility of having to pay for the Windsor Castle restoration brought the announcement forward.

It was also announced that official funding for the royal family would be limited to the Queen, Prince Philip and the Queen Mother. The payments for Princess Anne, Prince Andrew, Prince Edward and Princess Margaret would be reimbursed to the government from the Queen's private funds.

Finally in April 1993 it was decided that the State Apartments of Buckingham Palace would be open to the paying public from that summer on an experimental basis, with the profits going towards the Windsor Castle repairs.

1994 marked the 25th anniversary of Prince Charles's Investiture at Caernarvon Castle. The prince authorised

the journalist Jonathan Dimbleby to produce a book and a TV programme that was initially to look at the prince's working life. After the Morton book and the collapse of the marriage in 1992, Charles was persuaded to change tack and to discuss more of his personal life.

On 29 June 1994, fourteen million people watched the prince confess to adultery on national television. Dimbleby asked: "did you try to be faithful and honourable to your wife when you took on the vow of marriage?"

"Yes" said the prince, "until it became irretrievably broken down, us both having tried."

More revelations emerged when the authorised biography was serialised in mid-October. In it the Queen was said to have been "detached" as a mother and that she and the Duke were "unable or unwilling" to give their eldest son "the affection and appreciation" he needed.

As with the Morton book, once again the timing was particularly unfortunate for the Queen. She and Prince Philip were en route to Russia for one of the most historic visits of her reign. There were strong family links with the Romanov dynasty. The Emperor Nicholas II was a first cousin of the Queen's grandfather, George V, and his wife, the Empress Alexandra, was Philip's great-aunt. Memories of the brutal murder of the Imperial family in July 1918 were still too raw for the British royals to visit during the Soviet era.

Elizabeth II spent the night in the Kremlin, emerging early the following day to take some personal snaps for her album, before her official tour later in the day. She went on to St Petersburg where she hosted a banquet for the ebullient Russian leader, Boris Yeltsin, on board the Royal Yacht *Britannia*.

The following March there was another historic tour when the Queen visited post-apartheid South Africa as a guest of Nelson Mandela, who had been elected President the previous April. The two had met at the Commonwealth Conference in Zambia in 1991 and had enjoyed an immediate rapport. Mandela has been the only non-royal leader to get away with calling the Queen "dear Elizabeth" to her face as well as on paper.

Prince Philip served in the war and the Queen joined the ATS in the final months of the conflict. Here she is seen walking through the British Military Cemetery in Bayeux, France during ceremonies honouring veterans and war dead on the 50th anniversary of D-Day. June 6, 1994.

(Opposite) Three years later the Queen made a historic visit to South Africa, her first since 1947. Here she talks to President Nelson Mandela in Cape Town. The two leaders formed a close relationship and Mandela was the only world leader who called her 'Elizabeth.'

To mark the 50th anniversary of VE Day the Queen and Princess Margaret joined their mother on the balcony of Buckingham Palace to replicate the famous photograph of them with Winston Churchill and the King at the end of hostilities. Here they watch a procession of vintage aircraft fly over the palace. May 8, 1995.

(Opposite) From the past to the future. The Queen launches the Royal website during a visit to Kingsbury High School in Brent. March 1997.

In May 1995 there were lavish celebrations in Britain to mark the 50th anniversary of the end of the Second World War in Europe. The Queen, Princess Margaret and the ninety-five-year-old Queen Mother emerged on to the palace balcony to recreate that famous photograph of them with the King and Churchill on VE Day. It had been the first major test of public affection since the events of 1992 and the Queen was moved to tears by the euphoria of the vast crowd that filled The Mall below her.

Diana played a full part in the events joining Prince Charles and their two sons for a celebratory gathering of veterans in Hyde Park in May and joining the royal party for a similar event to mark the anniversary of VJ Day in August.

No one had an inkling in the ensuing months that the princess was planning another bombshell that was to be far more explosive than the Morton book. She privately agreed to film an hour-long documentary for the BBC's *Panorama*. She kept her own staff, friends and advisers in the dark and the production crew, led by interviewer Martin Bashir, pointedly failed to inform senior executives including the Chairman, Marmaduke Hussey, whose wife, Lady Susan, was a lady-in-waiting and close friend of the Queen's.

A TV audience of just under 23 million watched in fascination as Diana, looking emotionally wrought-up, declared: "there were three of us in this marriage, so it got pretty crowded." She admitted to her own infidelity saying of James Hewitt: "yes, I loved him. I adored him... and he let me down."

Probably the most damaging fallout for the royal family was when she said she did not expect Charles to succeed as king.

The Queen decided enough was enough and, after consulting the Prime Minister and the Archbishop of Canterbury, she wrote to both the prince and the princess pointing out firmly that in her opinion an early divorce settlement was now the only solution. The couple began divorce proceedings almost immediately and their fifteen-year marriage finally ended in August 1996.

In 1996 the Queen reached her 70th birthday but declined any public celebrations, settling for a private

dinner with her family at Frogmore House in the grounds of Windsor Great Park. She was in the peak of health and that year undertook more official engagements than she had done twenty years earlier.

During her reign the Queen has more often than not been pragmatic about change and the need to modernise the monarchy. Her advisers were keen to keep apace with changes in technology and in 1997 Buckingham Palace went onto the Net.

The Queen unveiled her website – www.royal.gov.uk – in person during a visit to Kingsbury High School on 6 March 1997. The site proved popular, with 12.5 million hits in the first two months.

There was change of a different kind in May of the same year, when the Labour Party won the General Election with the greatest landslide victory since the Second World War. Tony Blair was Elizabeth II's tenth Prime Minister and the first to have been born during her reign. It was a reminder of the passage of time, since Winston Churchill, her first premier, fought for Queen Victoria at the Battle

of Omdurman in 1898 whereas Tony Blair was born four weeks before her Coronation in 1953.

At the beginning of her reign she was dealing with courtiers and politicians who were mostly from her parents' generation and beyond. By the late 90s most of her key staff were twenty years her junior and increasingly it was the Queen who was giving advice and guidance rather than the other way round. Then suddenly, in the summer of 1997, an unlikely chain of events gave rise to the second major crisis faced by the monarchy in just five years, leaving the Queen feeling vulnerable.

Shortly before one o'clock on the morning of 31 August, Robin Janvrin, the Queen's Deputy Private Secretary, was awoken by a telephone call from the British Ambassador in Paris to say that the Princess of Wales and her new love, Dodi Fayed, had been injured in a car crash.

Janvrin was on duty at Balmoral Castle where the Queen and several members of her family were on their annual summer break. He promptly telephoned the Queen and Prince Charles in their rooms to tell them the news.

It soon emerged that Dodi and the driver, Henri Paul, were dead, but initially it was thought Diana would survive. Eventually another call just before 4am broke the news that she had died, having suffered severe internal injuries.

The Queen was shocked and devastated and her first reaction was for her grandsons. "We must get the radios out of their rooms," she said to Charles. She also felt it was better the boys should be allowed to sleep through until the morning, and to be told the news after a good night's sleep.

From her earliest years the Queen was taught to hide personal pain and sadness behind an inscrutable exterior. Her personal mantra has always been to carry on as normal no matter what.

While the nation was reeling on hearing the terrible news, senior members of the royal family prepared to attend the usual Sunday morning service at Crathie Kirk where the news that was on everyone's lips was not even mentioned by the minister.

The Queen is greeted by the Dean as she arrives at Westminster Abbey for the funeral of Diana, Princess of Wales. September 6, 1997.

(Opposite) The Queen had been due to travel to London on Saturday morning but had changed her plans when it became imperative for her to broadcast to the nation on the eve of the ceremony. Here she leaves Aberdeen airport on the afternoon of Friday September 5.

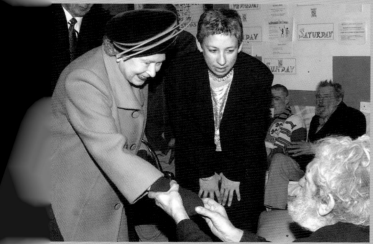

In the aftermath of Diana's death, the Queen's advisers tried to update the monarch's image with a new style, less traditional approach to engagements.

(Top Left) The Queen alighted from her car outside a McDonalds drive-through restaurant at Cheshire Oaks Designer Outlet village in Ellesmere Port, near Liverpool, July 1998.

(right) The Queen holds a bottle of beer presented to her at the Bridge Inn in Topsham, Devon in March of the same year.

(Left) Meeting residents of the Crisis homeless shelter in Southwark on New Year's Eve 1999.

(Opposite) The Queen and Duke of Edinburgh leave the Royal Yacht *Britannia* for the last time in Portsmouth during its decommissioning ceremony. Elizabeth memorably shed a tear in public as the end of the short service, December 11, 1997.

During the ensuing days, as a wave of emotion was whipped up into a maelstrom by the media, the apparent indifference shown by the monarch and her family to the nation's grief became the overriding theme in newspaper coverage.

The Queen and her advisers decided something had to be done and a live broadcast was set up for the evening before Diana's funeral from Buckingham Palace. In a highly personal address the monarch told her grieving people: "what I say to you now, as your Queen and a grandmother, I say from my heart."

This and her earlier walkabout among the crowds outside the palace as well as her willingness to change precedent and to order the lowering of the Union flag above the palace on the day of the funeral, undoubtedly helped diffuse some of the anger and tension that was reaching fever pitch.

The Queen and Prince Philip celebrated their Golden Wedding on 20 November 1997 and it was an opportunity for the normally reticent couple to pay public tribute to each other. The day before, at a banquet in London's Guildhall, the Duke said that tolerance is the key to a successful marriage, adding: "You can take it from me that the Queen has it in abundance."

On the actual anniversary, and at another lunch, this time hosted by Tony Blair at Banqueting House in Whitehall, the Queen praised her husband. "He is someone who doesn't take easily to compliments," she told guests, "but he has, quite simply, been my strength and stay all these years, and I, and his whole family, and this and many other countries, owe him a debt greater than he would ever claim, or we shall ever know".

The year ended on a sad note with the decommissioning ceremony for the Royal Yacht *Britannia* at Portsmouth. Fourteen members of the royal family were present and the Queen paid tribute to the yacht and those who had served with her. "Looking back over 44 years," said Her Majesty, "we can all reflect with pride and gratitude upon this great ship which has served the country, the Royal Navy and my family with such distinction." The normally impassive monarch famously shed a tear as the ship's company saluted her at the conclusion of the event.

Following the death of Diana, the Queen's advisers began to alter the way her royal engagements were structured to bring in a new approach, to show Her Majesty was willing to embrace change. Theme days were created during which the Queen and her family would highlight one particular industry or profession. Over the years these have focused on a wide variety of areas from the theatre to the navy, and from bookselling to the financial institutions of the City.

Stage-managed photo opportunities showed the Queen visiting a pub, meeting locals outside a drive-in McDonald's and having her hands massaged by an aromatherapist in a community centre. The message was clear; the Diana-effect had not gone unnoticed in royal circles.

The decade ended with another royal wedding. In June 1999 Prince Edward married Sophie Rhys-Jones, the chairman of a PR Company who been dating the prince since 1993. Instead of a traditional Abbey wedding, the couple opted for St George's Chapel, Windsor, and in another break with the recent past, decided on a late afternoon ceremony with guests in evening dress, followed by a buffet meal in the State Apartments.

It was another royal romance that increasingly dominated the headlines at the turn of the century. Prince Charles had declared his long-term love, Camilla Parker-Bowles, to be a 'non-negotiable' part of his life. Sensitivity about the fall-out from the death of Diana had prevented the couple appearing in public.

By 1999 the prince and his advisers felt the time was right for Mrs Parker Bowles to appear at a public event with the prince. On 28 January the two were photographed together, leaving the Ritz Hotel, by a massive press contingent following the 50th birthday party for Camilla's sister Annabel Elliot.

In June of 2000 the Queen formally met Camilla at a 60th birthday party for ex-King Constantine of Greece, hosted by Prince Charles at Highgrove. The two had a brief

but cordial chat and afterwards sat at the same table. As Supreme Governor of the Church of England, the Queen has always been uncomfortable about the remarriage of divorcees, but she had begun to realise that the prince was never going to change his mind about the relationship.

The Queen saw in the new century at the official opening of the ill-fated £758 million Millennium Dome in Greenwich, during which she linked hands with her husband and Tony Blair in an awkward rendition of *Auld Lang Syne*.

Earlier in the day she had visited Southwark Cathedral for a service reflecting the religious significance of the celebrations. She also met some of the poorest people in the same borough of London at a nearby homeless hostel.

2000 would see four special landmark birthdays for the Queen's family. Prince Andrew was 40 in February, Princess Anne was 50 in August, Princess Margaret was 70 in the same month and the seemingly indomitable Queen Mother reached her century. On the actual day – 4 August – the Queen sent her mother a telegram of congratulations.

(Clockwise from top) On her birthday the Queen Mother travelled to Buckingham Palace in a decorated carriage before appearing on the balcony with her daughters.

(Below Right) Six days before the Queen Mother's 100th birthday she attended Ascot races with the Queen for the De Beers Diamond Day including the King George VI and Queen Elizabeth Diamond Stakes. July 29, 2000.

(Below left) As a birthday treat the royal party went to London's Covent Garden to see the Kirov Ballet dance a mixed programme by the legendary Russian choreographer Mikhail Fokine.

(Opposite) The Queen on the steps of St George's Chapel, Windsor for the wedding of her third son Prince Edward to Sophie Rhys-Jones. June 1999.

The Queen was accompanied by the US Ambassador William Farish (top left) and his wife (top centre) and the Duke of Edinburgh (top centre right) for the service of remembrance at St Paul's Cathedral, London. September 14, 2001.

(Opposite) At another service this time at St Paul's Church in Canberra, Australia during the Queen's March 2000 tour. Here she meets Aboriginal didgeridoo player Robert Slockee after he played for her.

Later the royal matriarch appeared on the balcony of Buckingham Palace to the cheers of hundreds of thousands of well-wishers gathered in the Mall.

In March 2000 the Queen visited Australia, some four months after a referendum had voted in favour of retaining the monarchy. In a conciliatory speech, Her Majesty declared: "the future of the monarchy in Australia is an issue for you, the Australian people, and you alone to decide by democratic and constitutional means. It should not be otherwise."

In June 2001 Prince Philip celebrated his 80th birthday in a typically low-key way. After a service of thanksgiving at St George's Chapel, Windsor, family and friends, together with representatives from some of the organizations he is connected with, gathered for a reception in the State Apartments.

Three months later, the Queen attended another major

religious service for an altogether different reason.

On 11 September 2001, like millions of others, the Queen watched, transfixed, the television coverage of the attacks on the World Trade Center. In her own words she was "in total shock" and felt "growing disbelief."

She immediately asked her Private Secretary to make it known she would attend a service at St Paul's Cathedral to honour the dead and wounded. She also authorised the playing of the American national anthem during the next Changing of the Guard ceremony at Buckingham Palace.

The Queen did what she does so very well, represented her country and its people with quiet, understated dignity. The following year would mark the 50th anniversary of her accession and it was an opportunity for Britain and the Commonwealth to thank her for half a century of hard work and selfless devotion.

Crowning Glory

For the Queen, jewels are the tools of her trade.
From the Imperial State Crown to her favourite
pearl necklace they help to define her image.

St Edward's Crown

The St Edward's Crown was refurbished from an older crown for the coronation of Charles II in 1661 and has been used to crown monarchs ever since, including Elizabeth II in 1953. It weighs 4 pounds and 12 ounces and, being of solid gold, is so heavy that it is only used for that one occasion. Along with the Imperial State Crown, this is kept with the Crown Jewels in the Tower of London.

Imperial State Crown

The Imperial State Crown is the best known of the royal crowns. It was made for Queen Victoria's coronation in 1838 and replicated for George VI in 1937. The arches were lowered for the coronation of 1953. It weighs 2 pounds and 13 ounces and is set with over 3,000 precious stones. Among the best known are St Edward's Sapphire (at the top of the crown), the Second Star of Africa (at the front of the band) and the Black Prince's Ruby (also at the front) which in fact is a spinel rather than a ruby. Pearls belonging to Elizabeth I are suspended from the middle of the crown. Apart from the coronation this is worn by the Queen at the State Opening of Parliament.

King George IV State Diadem

The King George IV State Diadem is, these days, only worn by women. The Queen inherited it in 1952 and wears it for the journey to and from Westminster for the State Opening of Parliament. She also wears it for official portraits and on some coins and stamp designs.

'Granny's Tiara'

This diamond tiara was originally made in 1893 for the wedding of the Queen's grandmother Queen Mary, who gave it to Elizabeth as a wedding present in 1947. Known as 'Granny's tiara' it is very light and feminine and is reckoned to be the Queen's favourite.

Grand Duchess Vladimir of Russia's Tiara

The Queen wore the Grand Duchess Vladimir of Russia's Tiara at this banquet in Lithuania in 2008. The tiara was smuggled out of Russia in 1919 just after the Revolution and was bought, two years later, by Britain's Queen Mary. Mary had it adapted so that the suspended pearls can be replaced with emeralds. She bequeathed it to her granddaughter in her will.

Here on her 2002 visit to Canada the Queen wears the Grand Duchess Vladimir Tiara with the Cambridge emeralds suspended from the diamond mount. On this occasion she has chosen to team it with some striking gold and emerald earrings and a matching necklace.

Diamond & Ruby Tiara

This diamond and ruby tiara, worn here for a State Banquet in Slovenia in 2008, was designed for the Queen in 1973 and made up of diamonds, from an older tiara, and rubies, given to her as a wedding present from the people of Burma.

The Indian Tiara

This diamond and ruby tiara was a favourite of the Queen Mother's and originally belonged to Queen Victoria. Here the Queen wears it at a State Dinner in Valletta, Malta in November 2005

Queen Alexandra's Russian Tiara

Another royal favourite is Queen Alexandra's Russian Tiara made for Elizabeth's great grandmother, Alexandra in 1888 as a Silver Wedding Present. It was made in the shape of a traditional Russian peasant girl's headdress and is totally encrusted with 488 diamonds.

Coronation Circlets

For her father's Coronation in 1937 Elizabeth and her sister Margaret wore simple lightweight circlets of silver gilt, fashioned in the form of miniature medieval crowns and ornamented with Maltese crosses and fleur-de-lys. The eleven-year-old princess only wore it on this one occasion.

The Queen waves to the crowd as she rides in the Gold State coach from Buckingham Palace to St Paul's Cathedral for a service of Thanksgiving to celebrate her Golden Jubilee. June 4, 2002.

Happy & Glorious

2002 – 2012

The Queen's sixth decade as monarch
began on a sad note with the deaths
of both her mother and her sister.

Happy & Glorious

The Queen's sixth decade as monarch began on a sad note with the deaths of both her mother and her sister within seven weeks of each other.

There was rejoicing with the hugely popular Golden Jubilee in 2002 and the Queen and Duke's Diamond Wedding anniversary five years later.

There were two very significant weddings. In 2005 Prince Charles married his long-term love, Camilla Parker Bowles, and in 2011, the Queen's grandson Prince William married his girlfriend of eight years, Catherine Middleton.

Not only were both unions great love matches, but also, more crucially for Elizabeth and the monarchy, they were a stabilising factor. In 2002 the Queen was 76 and the personal relationship between Charles and Camilla had yet to be formalised and William, then aged 20, had not yet had a steady girlfriend. A decade on and both the future Charles V and William III have loving, supportive consorts whom the public have increasingly warmed to. For the Queen 'the firm', as she calls the monarchy, couldn't be in better shape.

The Queen spent the fiftieth anniversary of her accession to the throne, 6 February 2002, by opening a £1.2 million cancer care and treatment centre at a hospital in King's Lynn, Norfolk.

It was regarded as a tribute to her father, George VI, who had died of cancer on that day in 1952, while staying at Sandringham

His widow, Queen Elizabeth the Queen Mother, for whom the day marked fifty years of widowhood, was still staying at the royal residence and had not been seen in public since before Christmas.

On a happier note, the palace released a series of photos of new portraits of the Queen and Duke taken by eleven

photographers, including the Duke of York, Lord Lichfield, fashion photographer Rankin and the Canadian musician Bryan Adams.

Three days after the official start to the Jubilee Year, a statement was released from Buckingham Palace: "The Queen, with great sadness, has asked for the following announcement to be made immediately".

"Her beloved sister, Princess Margaret, died peacefully in her sleep this morning at 6:30am in the King Edward VII Hospital."

The princess had suffered a series of strokes, the first whilst on holiday in the Caribbean in 1998. She had also suffered severe burns to her feet when she scalded them while again on holiday in Mustique. The day before her death she suffered a final stroke, which led to cardiac problems during the night.

In a TV Broadcast Prince Charles described his "darling aunt" as "such a wonderfully vibrant woman with such a free spirit," adding "the last few years with her awful illness were hard for her to deal with."

Her funeral was held at St George's Chapel, Windsor, the following Friday. Her 101-year-old mother made a supreme effort to attend, against doctor's orders. It was her final public appearance. The princess was later cremated at Slough Crematorium and her ashes were interred in the tomb of her parents.

The Queen Mother stayed on at Royal Lodge in Windsor Great Park and passed away peacefully on the afternoon of Saturday 30 March 2002. It was Easter Saturday and the Queen, who was in residence at Windsor Castle, spent the afternoon at her mother's bedside and was holding her hand when she died.

Once again Prince Charles paid a moving tribute. His grandmother, he said, "was the original life enhancer… at once indomitable, somehow timeless, able to span

The Queen's sixth decade as sovereign began with great personal loss when both her sister and mother died within weeks of each other. Here a bereft looking Elizabeth acknowledges the crowds as she is driven back to Buckingham Palace after a ceremonial procession had taken the Queen Mother's coffin to Westminster Hall in central London. April 5, 2002.

(Opposite) The Queen stands with her nephew Viscount Linley and niece Lady Sarah Chatto as they watch Princess Margaret's coffin leave St George's Chapel, Windsor, following her funeral. February 15, 2002.

The Queen and Prince Philip spent the Golden Jubilee year of 2002 travelling extensively throughout Britain and the Commonwealth.

(Top Left) She was clearly delighted with her reception at the Hugh Sherlock School in Trenchtown, Jamaica. February 19, 2002.

(Top right) Two week's later and the royal couple were in Australia where they were entertained at Tjapukai Aboriginal Culture Park in Cairns.

(Left) The Queen wore her own kiwi feather korowai (cloak) given to her for her Coronation in 1953, when she joined tribal Head, Rick Te-Tau, at the Marae (meeting house) of the Ngai Tahu Maori tribe in Rehua, a region of Christchurch, New Zealand. February 25, 2002.

(Opposite) The Queen and Prince Philip accompanied by the Superintendent of Windsor Castle, Munro Davidson (centre), look at flowers left in the castle grounds by well wishers following the death of the Queen Mother. April 4, 2002.

the generations; wise, loving, and an utterly irresistible mischievousness of spirit".

"She was quite simply the most magical grandmother you could possibly have, and I was utterly devoted to her".

The Queen Mother's body lay in state in Westminster Hall prior to her funeral service in Westminster Abbey on 9 April and a private interment at Windsor.

On the eve of the funeral the Queen also broadcast to the nation, thanking the public for their "deeply moving" and "overwhelming" tributes to her mother.

She said: "I have drawn great comfort from so many individual acts of kindness and respect."

It was perhaps partly due to the deaths of the Queen's sister and mother that, during this Jubilee year of 2002, there was such a huge outpouring of affection for Elizabeth, who was now the last survivor of "we four", as her father called his immediate family.

From February to October, the Queen and the Duke of Edinburgh undertook a wide-ranging programme, beginning with a tour of the Caribbean, Australia and New Zealand and ending with a visit to Canada.

She and the Duke, then aged 81, travelled a total of 40,000 miles in the UK and overseas. In Britain alone they visited 70 cities and towns in 50 counties in England, Scotland, Wales and Northern Ireland over 38 days from May to August.

During this Jubilee year of 2002, there was such a huge outpouring of affection for Elizabeth, who was now the last survivor of "we four" as her father called his immediate family.

During the Jubilee weekend two public concerts were held in the gardens of Buckingham Palace. The pop concert alone attracted 200 million viewers from all over the world.

On 4 June the entire royal family attended a national Thanksgiving Service at St Paul's Cathedral, to which the Queen travelled in the Gold State Coach. Afterwards there was a lunch at the Guildhall, followed by a Jubilee Parade down the Mall.

Finally the Queen made an appearance on a specially decorated palace balcony. As she turned to go inside it was noted that she had tears in her eyes at the tumultuous reception she had received.

In January 2003, the Queen was admitted to the King Edward VII Hospital in London where she had keyhole surgery on her right knee. The 76-year-old monarch had experienced discomfort and had to walk with a stick after wrenching her knee walking on uneven ground during a private visit to Newmarket a week earlier. A scan later revealed a torn cartilage.

The operation was carried out under a general anaesthetic but she was able to leave less than a day later for a two-week recovery at Sandringham.

Eleven months later, she returned to the same hospital to have torn cartilage removed from her other knee and what were described as "benign skin lesions" removed from her face.

In June 2003 the Queen hosted a 21st birthday party for Prince William in the State Apartments at Windsor Castle. They were transformed into scenes from the African bush, which include a life-sized elephant made out of *papier-mâché*, and African band Shakarimba had been flown in especially from Botswana where William had heard them while on holiday. The prince wore a lion skin and even the Queen was in costume.

300 guests were invited to the party but 301 arrived thanks to the presence of gate-crasher Aaron Barschak of London, the self-proclaimed 'comedy terrorist.' He managed to evade the elaborate security arrangements and might well have spent the whole evening undetected had he not stumbled on stage and grabbed the microphone while

The highlight of the Golden Jubilee year was the Thanksgiving service at St Paul's Cathedral on June 4, 2002. Here the Queen rides in the Gold State coach from Buckingham Palace to St Paul's Cathedral. Built for King George III in 1762, she had only used the coach twice before, for her Coronation, and her Silver Jubilee.

(Opposite) the 76-year-old monarch visited every region of the United Kingdom during her jubilee year. Here she greets well-wishers at Falmouth harbour during a two-day visit to the West Country. May 1, 2002.

The Queen has met eleven US Presidents face to face. Here she acknowledges well-wishers from the balcony of the White House where she was a guest of President George W. Bush and his wife Laura during her state visit to America. May 7, 2007.

(Opposite) George Bush Jnr became the first US President to stay at Buckingham Palace, where he attended a state banquet hosted by the Queen on the first day of his visit. November 19, 2003.

the prince was thanking his father and the Queen for organising the party.
He was immediately pounced on by security guards and police before being taken off to a Thames Valley police station for questioning.

Mr Barschak's father Fred told BBC News his son was trying to get publicity ahead of performing at the Edinburgh festival. He said "I think it's a high price to pay for publicity."

Ahead of the birthday, William gave an interview during which he dispelled rumours that he didn't want to be king. He also praised Prince Charles and defended his reputation.

"He does so many amazing things, I only wish people would see that more because he's had a very hard time and yet he's stuck it out and he's still very positive."

William added: "He's very happy and protective towards Harry and me as well."

In November it was revealed that there had been another unwelcome intruder on royal property. Ryan Parry, a reporter from the *Daily Mirror*, had been working undetected for two months as a footman at Buckingham Palace.

His story only came to light when the tabloid revealed Parry's palace secrets in a 15-page feature including photos snapped by the 'footman' himself. The bedroom shared by the Earl and Countess of Wessex showed they like to adorn it with furry bears and dogs. There were more stuffed toys shown in the Duke of York's apartment, together with a cushion bearing the woven message, "Eat, sleep and remarry."

The main talking point afterwards was a photo of the Queen's breakfast table. Rather than eating surrounded by gold and silver, the monarch has her cornflakes and porridge sealed in Tupperware containers. The Queen and Duke have a Roberts radio on the table as well a choice of light and dark marmalade and a carton of yoghurt.

In the long term the exposé worked in the Queen's

favour as it added to her image as a down-to-earth figure, with a practical approach to life. Unsurprisingly sales of Tupperware soared in the aftermath.

In the short-term of course the story showed how lax the palace vetting system was at the time, since Ryan managed to secure the job using a fake reference. The Prime Minister, Tony Blair, asked the Security Commission, headed by Dame Elizabeth Butler-Sloss, to conduct an inquiry into the scandal.

It was all the more embarrassing as George W Bush was that week due to arrive for a State Visit and to become the first US President to stay at the palace.

Gaffe-prone George 'Dubya' Bush first met the Queen on her 1991 visit to his parents. Introduced over tea, he said: "I'm the black sheep of the family. Who's yours?" His mother, Barbara, swiftly stepped in and warned the monarch, "Don't answer that."

In May 2007 the Queen paid a return visit. In his welcoming speech outside the White House Mr Bush came up trumps again by misreading his notes and announcing she had toured the States in 1776 rather than 1976. Instead of swiftly moving on, he turned to give her a sly wink before reporting: "she gave me a look that only a mother could give a child!"

Just before the Bush visit to the UK, the Queen became a grandmother for the seventh time, when her daughter-in-law Sophie Wessex gave birth prematurely to a daughter, on 8 November 2003 shortly after 9:30pm.

It was a worrying time for all concerned since Sophie suffered a placental abruption, causing severe blood loss, and had to be rushed to Frimley Park Hospital in Surrey for an emergency Caesarean section. The Countess had previously suffered an ectopic pregnancy.

The baby was transferred to St George's Hospital, Tooting as a precaution and wasn't released until 23 November.

She was baptised Louise Alice Elizabeth Mary in the Private Chapel at Windsor Castle. Among her godparents was Lady Sarah Chatto, the Queen's niece. As a daughter of one of the Queen's sons she had the right to be known as HRH Princess Louise, but her parents decided against this. One possible reason, suggested at the time, was that as eighth in line to the throne, it would be unlikely she would be needed to carry out royal engagements in the future, especially when William and Harry have their own families.

On 17 December 2007 the Queen's eighth grandchild was born, when Sophie gave birth to a son, James Alexander Philip Theo, Viscount Severn. Prince Edward, who was present at the birth, described it as "a lot calmer than last time" (a reference to the emergency delivery of their first child, Lady Louise), and that his son was: "like most babies, rather small, very cute and very cuddly."

At the time of his wedding in 1999 it was announced that Prince Edward would be known as Earl of Wessex but in the fullness of time would succeed his father as Duke of Edinburgh. Thus James will eventually become the 3rd Duke of Edinburgh in its modern creation.

2004 was the centenary of the *Entente Cordiale* between Britain and France that was largely the brainchild of Elizabeth's francophile great grandfather, King Edward VII.

To mark the occasion, in April the Queen travelled by Eurostar to Paris to begin a State Visit hosted by President Chirac.

In November, the French President returned the visit and was entertained with a special performance by the London cast of *Les Misérables*. The setting was the Waterloo Chamber at Windsor Castle.

The chamber was built to commemorate the famous British victory over Napoleon and is adorned with the portraits of heads of state and military leaders who defeated him. Diplomatically it was rebranded as 'The Music Room' for this one-off occasion.

Four years later Chirac's successor, Nicolas Sarkozy, was also a guest at Windsor Castle, during his State Visit to the UK in March 2008 with his then new wife, Carla Bruni-Sarkozy, whom he had married the previous month.

In a later interview the French President, who is teetotal, revealed he took what he thought was a glass of water, only to find it was gin.

The effect, he said, was immediate. "It was when I asked the Queen whether she ever got bored and she replied, 'Yes but I don't say so', that I understood I'd been drinking," he told journalists.

In the same month as the Chirac visit there was another reminder of past enmity when the Queen and Duke paid a State Visit to Germany. The mass-circulation tabloid *Bild* suggested that she say sorry for the destruction of Dresden by allied bombers.

Instead the Queen spoke of the need for "reconciliation" between the two countries. Speaking at a banquet hosted by President Horst Köhler she said: "In remembering the appalling suffering of war on both sides, we recognise how precious is the peace we have built in Europe since 1945."

The French President, who is teetotal, revealed he took what he thought was a glass of water, only to find it was gin.

(Above) The Queen and the President Nicolas Sarkozy attend a State Banquet at Windsor Castle during the French state visit. Behind them Prince Philip escorts Carla Bruni-Sarkozy. March 25, 2008.

(Inset) Guiding her guests from the ceremonial dais after the review of the Guard of Honour.

(Opposite) Stepping off the Eurostar at Gare du Nord station in Paris, at the start of her official state visit to France. She and the Duke of Edinburgh left London Waterloo at 11:13am on a special charter service for a three-day tour to mark the 100th anniversary of Entente Cordiale. April 5, 2004.

Happy Families. The official wedding photo of the Prince of Wales and his new bride Camilla, Duchess of Cornwall, with their families (L-R back row Prince Harry, Prince William, Tom and Laura Parker Bowles (L-R front row) Duke of Edinburgh, The Queen and Camilla's father Major Bruce Shand, in the White Drawing Room at Windsor Castle. April 9, 2005.

(Opposite) Happy and glorious on a walkabout in Windsor High Street on her 80th birthday. April 21, 2006.

A string of family celebrations dominated the middle years of the Queen's sixth decade as monarch. In April 2005 the Prince of Wales married Camilla Parker Bowles in the Guildhall at Windsor. The preparations had been fraught with problems. The civil wedding had been due to be held in the state apartments of Windsor Castle until it was discovered that licensing the venue for such weddings would require opening it up to other couples for at least three years.

It was stated that the Queen would not attend the wedding ceremony but would attend the blessing in St George's Chapel before hosting a reception.

One final problem came in the immediate run-up to the wedding when it was announced from the Vatican that the funeral of Pope John Paul II would be held on 8 April, obliging the prince to postpone his wedding by 24 hours so as not to conflict with the funeral and also so he could attend as the Queen's representative.

The Queen stole the show at the reception with an hilarious speech comparing his marriage to the Grand National.

The racing mad monarch started with: "I've got two things to announce to you of the greatest importance."

Then, to peals of laughter, she added: "The first is that the Grand National was won by Hedgehunter. The second is to say to you that, despite Becher's Brook and The Chair and all kinds of other terrible obstacles, my son has come through and I'm very proud and wish them well. The couple have finally arrived in the Winners' enclosure."

The following April the Queen celebrated her 80th birthday with an informal walkabout in Windsor. The band of the Irish Guards played *Happy Birthday* as she emerged from the Henry VIII Gate of Windsor Castle and accepted gifts and cards from some of the thousands crowding the narrow streets of the Berkshire town.

Three months later, the Queen chartered the MV *Hebridean Princess*, a luxury cruiser, for a celebratory cruise around the Western Isles of Scotland with members of her family. This used to be a regular occurrence each summer on board the Royal Yacht *Britannia*.

The cruise lasted eight days and all four of her children joined her for some or all of the holiday. Four years later she hired it once again at the same time of year to celebrate the 60th birthday of Princess Anne and the 50th birthday of Prince Andrew.

Over the years the Queen has occasionally attended the Sovereign's Parade at Sandhurst in person. On 2006 she attended twice. The first time in April to take the salute at Prince Harry's passing out ceremony and again in December for Prince William's.

In November 2007 the Queen and Duke celebrated their Diamond Wedding with a Thanksgiving Service at Westminster Abbey. A photo was released of them at Broadlands, the Hampshire home of the Mountbatten family, recreating honeymoon photos taken at the same venue in 1947.

On the actual day of the anniversary, 20 November, the couple flew to Malta, the island they lived on as newlyweds from 1949-51. They were due to be present at the Commonwealth Heads of Government Meeting in

Uganda and, in a romantic gesture, Prince Philip suggested the stop-over on the Mediterranean Island, though time constraints meant they only had one night there.

Elizabeth is the first British monarch to have celebrated a Diamond Wedding and during this decade she would also break other records. On 21 December 2007 she became the oldest reigning monarch, having outlived her great-great-grandmother, Queen Victoria, who died on 22 January 1901 aged 81 years, 7 months and 29 days.

On 12th May 2011 Queen Elizabeth II became the second longest reigning monarch in over a thousand years of British history. She will have to reign until 10th September 2015, when she will be 89 years old, to reign longer than her great-great-grandmother Queen Victoria, who reigned for 63 years and 216 days from 1837-1901.

In March 2008 the Queen paid a three-day visit to Northern Ireland and made history by attending the annual Royal Maundy service at St Patrick's Church of Ireland Cathedral in Armagh, the first time the service has been held outside England or Wales.

To mark their Diamond Wedding anniversary the Queen and Duke made a nostalgic return visit to Romsey Abbey in Hampshire where they spent the first part of their honeymoon. November 1947.

(Opposite) The royal couple with their four children at a family dinner hosted by Prince Charles at Clarence House to mark his parents' 60th wedding anniversary. November 18, 2007.

(Above) A photocall with US President Barack Obama and First Lady Michelle in the Music Room of Buckingham Palace ahead of a State Banquet, as part of the Presidents three-day state visit to the UK. May 24, 2011.

(Inset) Two years earlier the Obamas paid a courtesy call on the Queen at Buckingham Palace. April 1, 2009.

(Opposite) Visiting the Green Mosque and listening to readings from the Koran on a visit to Bursa, in during the State Visit to Turkey. May 2008.

Two months later she visited Turkey for the first time since 1971, at a time when the British Government was supporting that country's bid to join the EU. During a State Banquet she described Turkey as: "a bridge between East and West at a crucial time." Earlier she had laid a wreath at the tomb of Mustafa Kemal Atatürk, the founder of the modern-day state. The Queen called him: "one of the greatest figures of modern history" and wrote in the mausoleum's visitors' book that it was an "honour" to pay her respects to "a much valued friend of the United Kingdom."

On the day after her return from Turkey, the Queen attended the wedding of her eldest grandson, Peter Phillips, to Canadian-born Autumn Kelly at St George's Chapel Windsor on 17 May 2008. Two years later the couple made the Queen a great grandmother when Autumn gave birth to a daughter, Savannah, on 29 December 2010. Elizabeth attended the baby's christening at Holy Cross Church, Avening, Gloucestershire, near the Princess Royal's estate, the following April.

It was announced in October 2011 that the couple are expecting their second child in March 2012. Fittingly this will be a Diamond Jubilee baby, since Peter was himself born in that other Jubilee year of 1977.

In April 2009 the Queen met the US President Barack Obama and his wife Michelle at Buckingham Palace. Like all his presidential predecessors Barack received silver framed signed photos of the Queen and Duke, but he was the first one to hand over an *iPod* in return. It was loaded with video footage and photos of Elizabeth's visit to Richmond, Jamestown and Williamsburg two years earlier. Presumably the monarch was too polite to tell him she already had a 6GB silver mini version bought by Prince Andrew in 2005.

Michelle struck up a warm relationship with the Queen. The two women joked about their height difference. As they moved closer together the Queen put her hand on the back of Mrs Obama who did the same for a few moments as they chatted. Michelle said ,"I really enjoyed our meeting," and the Queen responded by telling the First Lady: "Now we have met, would you please keep in touch?"

The two exchanged letters and phone calls and in June of the same year, Michelle called in again, this time with daughters Malia and Sasha. They were taken on a private tour of the palace and gardens before being joined by the Queen.

In May 2011 the Obamas visited the UK officially and were once again received at Buckingham Palace where this time they had a private audience with the recently married Duke and Duchess of Cambridge.

The Queen flew to New York in July 2010 after completing her 22nd tour of Canada. She was there to address the United Nations General Assembly for the first time since 1957. Elizabeth told the UN it had "moved from being a high-minded aspiration to being a real force for common good."

Her five-hour visit to New York included a stop at the World Trade Center site, laying a wreath in tribute to the thousands who died in the 9/11 attack, including 67 Britons. She then moved on to Hanover Square to officially open the British Garden of Remembrance and meet families of the British victims.

In the spring of 2010 Elizabeth and her advisers faced the possibility of having to involve the Queen in politics when the May General Election resulted in no overall majority for one party. This meant a 'hung parliament' and could have risked jeopardising the Queen's traditional political impartiality, had no solution to the crisis been found, and the monarch would have to decide who was best placed to form a government. In the event David Cameron, the Conservative Party leader, forged an alliance with the Liberal Democrats, giving Elizabeth the first coalition government of her reign.

Mr Cameron is the 12th Prime Minister since 1952 and is the first one of the Queen's reign to be younger than all four of her children.

The final year of Elizabeth's sixth decade as monarch was dominated by the royal wedding of her grandson Prince William to his girlfriend of eight years, Catherine Middleton. The Queen was hosting a reception at Windsor Castle the day the announcement of the couple's engagement was made. She told one guest: "It is brilliant news," adding, "It has taken them a very long time."

It was the first time a monarch has lived to see the wedding of a grandchild in direct succession to the throne since 1893 when Queen Victoria attended the marriage ceremony of her grandson the Duke of York, (later George V), who married Princess Mary of Teck.

On the morning of 29 April 2011 it was announced that the Queen had bestowed on William the title Duke of Cambridge, Earl of Strathearn and Baron Carrickfergus.

On the couple's engagement.
"It is brilliant news." adding,
"It has taken them a very long time."

(Above) Not centre stage for once; the Queen stands next to the pageboys on the balcony of Buckingham Palace following the wedding of Prince William and Catherine Middleton. April 29, 2011.

(Bottom Left) The Queen and the Duchess of Cornwall watch as the couple leave Westminster Abbey by carriage.

(Bottom Right) Perhaps sharing memories of their own wedding on the same spot 63 years earlier.

(Opposite) The Queen and her 12th Prime Minister, David Cameron, look at photos of some of the other holders of that office during her reign at a lunch at 10 Downing Street to mark Prince Philip's 90th birthday. June 21, 2011.

Wearing a dress decorated with over a thousand tiny shamrock and a brooch made of crystals in the shape of a harp, during a State Banquet held at Dublin Castle during the Queen's historic visit to Ireland. May 2011.

Later William revealed that he had asked his grandmother for advice on the guest list. Faced with a list of official names he ought to ask, but did not even recognise, he realised there was only one person who could resolve the issue - the Queen herself.

According to William: "I rang her up the next day and said: 'Do we need to be doing this?' And she said: 'No. Start with your friends first and then go from there.' And she told me to bin the list."

"She made the point that there are certain times when you have to strike the right balance. And it's advice like that, which is really key, when you know that she's seen and done it before."

After the ceremony the Queen hosted a lunchtime reception for 650 guests in the State Apartments before quietly leaving for a weekend away so that the younger generation could enjoy a dinner hosted by Prince Charles, followed by a party that went on into the night.

Three months later, the Queen hosted another wedding reception, this time for her eldest granddaughter Zara Phillips, who married her rugby-playing partner Mike Tindall. The ceremony took place at Canongate Kirk near to the Palace of Holyrood.

Zara wore a dress of ivory silk faille by Stewart Parvin, one of the Queen's favourite designers, and a diamond tiara that had belonged to Prince Philip's mother, Princess Andrew of Greece.

Between the two weddings Prince Philip marked his 90th birthday by attending a service at St George's Chapel Windsor in what was turning out to be a summer of celebrations.

Earlier in the year he had been by the Queen's side during her historic visit to Ireland, the first one to the republic since George V's 1911 stay.

The 4-day tour from 17 to 20 May was considered to be a diplomatic triumph. The Queen arrived at Casement military airbase wearing an emerald green coat and hat. There were more sartorial compliments at a state banquet when Elizabeth wore a white evening gown designed by her senior dresser, Angela Kelly, that was appliquéd with over 2,000 silk shamrocks. She also wore a brooch made from Swarovski crystals in the shape of an Irish harp.

One of the most talked about moments occurred when Her Majesty began her speech to the assembled dinner guests in their own language. As she flawlessly pronounced the words "A Uachtaráin agus a chairde," (President and friends) the Irish president, Mary McAleese, could be seen to mouth the word "wow" and there was a round of appreciative applause.

Another talked-about moment occurred when the British monarch bowed her head in Dublin's Garden of Remembrance in Parnell Square, which honours the patriots who died fighting for Irish freedom.

The Queen and Duke also visited Australia in October 2011 for an 11-day tour, taking in Canberra, Melbourne, Brisbane and Perth. As she prepared to leave for the UK after what many believe could be her final visit she said: "We have been overwhelmed by your kindness and support."

"Once again, we will return to the United Kingdom with fond memories of our time here and the warm Australian welcome we have received on our 16th visit to this beautiful country."

The year ended on a worrying note when the Duke of Edinburgh was taken ill with chest pains while preparing for Christmas at Sandringham. An RAF helicopter took him to Papworth hospital near Cambridge where a coronary stent was fitted. The Queen visited him on Christmas Eve and on Christmas Day his six eldest grandchildren drove the 90 minute round trip from Sandringham to see him. After a four-night stay he returned to join his family to resume the Christmas break and walked the quarter of a mile to St Mary Magdalene Church on New Year's Day.

For the Queen the end of her sixth decade on the throne saw the monarchy in a much stronger position than it has been for over two decades. The marriages of princes Charles and William have stabilised what the Queen calls 'the firm' and the addition of the glamorous Duchess of Cambridge augurs well for the future.

Queen Elizabeth II attends a reception at Holyrood Park in Scotland, after presenting the new Colours to the Royal Regiment of Scotland during a ceremony. July 2011.

Legacy

The Queen has been a constant in most of our lives for six decades.

She became Queen in February 1952, five and a half years after the end of World War II, at a time when Joseph Stalin was leading Russia, Harry S Truman was President of the USA and China was ruled by Chiang Kai-shek. Her own Prime Minister, Winston Churchill, had fought for Queen Victoria at the Battle of Omdurman in 1898.

2012 is a vastly different world and yet Elizabeth II still reigns and still works hard for Britain and its Commonwealth. Last year she carried out 370 engagements, some of which were during her landmark tour of Ireland in May and her sixteenth visit to Australia in October.

In addition there are briefings, dress fittings, portrait sittings and so on. There are also her red boxes containing papers from government departments in this country as well as the fifteen other states of which she is Queen.

During her six decades she has never shirked her responsibility or taken a sabbatical, even after giving birth to her two youngest children while she was monarch.

She is present at all the key ceremonies of the year from attending the Maundy Service at Easter to the Remembrance Service in November, from Trooping the Colour in June to the State Opening of Parliament. In addition she usually hosts two incoming State Visits a year and makes her own State Visit or Commonwealth visit as well.

The statistics for her body of work are staggering. She has been present at every Trooping the Colour apart from in 1955 when it was cancelled due to a rail strike, and has always opened parliament at Westminster in person apart from in 1959 and 1963 when she was pregnant with Andrew and Edward respectively.

We should not of course forget that most of these engagements are undertaken with the Duke of Edinburgh by her side. The Queen's reign has been, to all intents and purposes, a joint reign, with the Duke constantly on hand to help his wife whenever he can.

There have been changes over the years. The Queen has been pragmatic in her approach to her role and made efforts to modernise and adapt the monarchy, particularly after hostile criticism in the late 1950s and again after the death of Diana, Princess of Wales in 1997.

There have been technical innovations. The British monarchy has its own website and appears on Twitter, YouTube and Facebook. The Queen herself has a mobile phone and has been known to send text messages and emails.

She has helped make the monarchy more accessible, especially using the media. She embraced the television age, agreeing to have her Coronation broadcast live and, four years later, she allowed her annual Christmas broadcast to be filmed by the BBC. Then of course there have been landmark documentaries such as *Royal Family* in 1969 and *Elizabeth R* in 1992.

There have been personal celebrations as well as crises, all played out in the full glare of the media. Thankfully her family life no longer makes headlines for all the wrong reasons and she can be rightly proud of the younger generations of royals, who she has guided and nurtured and who in turn respect her wisdom and example.

In April 1947 Princess Elizabeth broadcast from Cape Town on her 21st Birthday. She vowed to serve Britain and its Empire for the rest of her life. It is a vow she has never broken and never will.

"He has, quite simply, been my strength and stay all these years." The Duke of Edinburgh has been by the Queen's side throughout her reign, attending all the key events of the royal year such as this Trooping the Colour ceremony. June 2011.

(Opposite) The Queen's Christmas Broadcast, one of the many traditions the Queen has upheld throughout her long reign. December 2011.

BIBLIOGRAPHY

Allison, Ronald	The Royal Encyclopedia	Macmillan
Bradford, Sarah	Elizabeth	Heinemann
Dimbleby, Jonathan	The Prince of Wales	Little Brown
Field, Leslie	The Queen's Jewels	Weidenfeld
Harris, Kenneth	The Queen	Weidenfeld
Heald, Tim	The Duke	Hodder
Lacey, Robert	Majesty	Random House
Lacey Robert	Royal	Little Brown
Longford, Elizabeth	Elizabeth R	Weidenfeld
Pimlott, Ben	The Queen	Harper Collins